The Antitrust Experiment In America

Donald Dewey

COLUMBIA UNIVERSITY PRESS
New York

Columbia University Press
New York   Oxford
Copyright © 1990 Columbia University Press

Library of Congress Cataloging-in-Publication Data

Dewey, Donald (Donald J.)
The antitrust experiment in America / Donald Dewey.
p.   cm.
Includes bibliographical references.
ISBN 0-231-06710-0
1. Trusts, Industrial—Government policy—United States—History.
2. Antitrust law—United States—History.
I. Title.
HD2795.D485   1990   67832
338.8'5'0973—dc20   90-30685
CIP

Casebound editions of Columbia University Press books are Smyth-sewn
and printed on permanent and durable acid-free paper

Printed in the United States of America

c 10 9 8 7 6 5 4 3 2 1

For Ruth

Contents

Preface

THE STUDIES that follow are a record of my interest in the problems of American antitrust policy extending over nearly four decades. As such, they form a very personal book but not, I believe, an especially egocentric or quixotic one. The issues examined have been widely studied and often fiercely debated in these years. Needing all the help I can get, my work has always relied heavily on that of others. Most of the changes in my thinking about antitrust that have occurred over the years are common to economists in my age cohort who had the good fortune to start out at the University of Chicago fifty years ago.

Most academics, I suspect, harbor the hope that their favorite professional papers will one day find a home in hardcovers. While I readily admit to this vanity, there are, I believe, more worthy reasons for bringing these studies together. Alfred Marshall once opined in good Victorian fashion that in economic matters mankind does not need to be instructed so much as it needs to be reminded. In antitrust matters the need for reminding is permanent and acute. The problems are many and some are extremely difficult. Most of us, at one time or another, bring to their study an encumbering baggage of emotions, methodological mind sets, and ideology that get in the way of clear thinking and accurate memory. To further muddy the waters, antitrust issues have long been discussed within the adversarial format imposed by the American legal system. The system may have much to recommend it as a way of determining guilt in criminal trials and liability in civil cases. It is far from ideal as a forum for scientific inquiry. My hope is that this book will help to preserve the intellectual wheat that has been painfully separated from the chaff over the years. Anyone who doubts the need for conservation is urged to read at random in the mountain of Congressional hearings, debates, and reports on changes in the antitrust laws that have been considered over the last century. It can be a very depressing experience.

The reader is free to regard the methodology of this book as either leavened or corrupted "Chicago economics." My formal study of economics began as an undergraduate on the Midway fifty years ago when the "Chicago School" was still infused with the skepticism and wide-ranging interests of Frank Knight and Jacob Viner, when Paul Douglas was teaching labor economics, and when introductory undergraduate instruction in economics was entrusted to Maynard Krueger—an avowed socialist. A totally undistinguished army career in World War II gained me the educational bounty of the G.I. Bill of blessed memory. It took me, in Spartan comfort, from the Midway to Cambridge and the London School of Economics by way of the Iowa State College, and the State University of Iowa where the fine teaching of Addison Hickman provided the last reason I needed to choose economics over law school. Not to overlook two pleasant summer schools, combined with a successful courtship, in Oxford; the G.I. Bill required that one had always to be enrolled somewhere in order to remain on the payroll. My travels concluded in 1949–50 with a year's fellowship back at Chicago and an office next to Milton Friedman's. (This took me off the government budget.)

The respect for formal price theory as a guide to economic consequences that was early acquired has remained a permanent possession; and the study of antitrust became a permanent interest when it proved to be a veritable Widow's Cruse of fascinating and challenging problems in price theory. (My recollection is that my introduction to antitrust issues came when, in my freshman year, I was put to read Henry Simons' *A Positive Program for Laissez Faire*.) Nevertheless, my education left me unwilling to confine my interest to antitrust viewed solely as a set of price theory problems or to believe that an antitrust rule must be accepted or rejected according to whether or not it can meet some strictly "economic" test.

Many colleagues, whether they knew it or not, have helped me on the road that led to this book and I have been able to enter a few, inadequate, acknowledgments along the way. Here a special thanks is due to a considerable multitude nowhere else mentioned—two generations of students at Duke and Columbia who bore with me every year in the industrial organization policy course while, as Frank Knight would say, I kept trying "to get it right." I like to believe that their reward was, beyond some useful drill in price theory and exposure to economic history, a better feel for how ideas, events, and hard slogging work by economists—and lawyers—have interacted to shape the antitrust policy of this country. Their reward certainly was not a fighting faith or a tidy set of class notes.

The previously published studies included in this volume are offered in their original form except for the correction of old typos, the introduction of new ones, and stylistic changes required by the standards of Columbia University Press. Nothing has been added save in the headnotes. Only two small excisions have been made. In chapter 2, a long footnote dealing with the Pullman and Paramount cases has been shortened as no longer being of topical interest. In chapter 6, a sentence that inaccurately summarized some empirical work of Joseph Seneca and Peter Asch has been eliminated. My decision to reprint with warts and all was not mainly dictated by sloth. Or so I believe. A major purpose of the book is to convey how the view of the "monopoly problem" of one pretty representative economist changed and, let us hope, evolved (in the biological sense) over the years.

The Antitrust Experiment in America

1.

The Antitrust Experiment, 1890–1990: A Judgment

O VER THE years the antitrust policy of the United States has inspired the emotions of veneration, contempt, incredulity, irritation, disappointment, and resignation. None of these reactions is wholly unreasonable. What has been constant since the coming of the Sherman Act[1] in 1890 is the policy's power to raise voices and tempers.

It is not that the importance of antitrust is self-evident. In its economic effects, insofar as they are known—a most important qualification as we shall see—antitrust ranks well below farm policy, monetary policy, tax policy, and even tariff policy. We have no solid evidence (as distinct from plausible armchair scenarios) to support the belief that the country would be perceptibly richer or poorer, the overall distribution of personal income different, or the quality of American political life better or worse had the antitrust experiment never been tried. Nor is antitrust an interesting area in which to study the interplay of special interest groups in American politics. It has been described, with only slight exaggeration, as a policy with-

For their help in getting my thoughts straight on this chapter, I would like to thank Bruce Bassett, Don Boudreaux, Stuart Bruchey, William Kenneth Jones, Olive Vaughan, and William Vickrey.
[1]26 Stat. 209 (1890).

out a constituency. In fact, it is this feature that makes antitrust so fascinating to anyone interested in the murky and complex process by which ideas shape policy and are, in turn, shaped by the results or, at any rate, the perceived results of policy.

Antitrust, of course, has a political constituency but, for better or worse, it is one of shared ideology (which is always some blend of ideals and perceptions of reality). Antitrust is *not* a policy that has endured and expanded for a century because it creates economic rents for important groups that defend it fiercely. The most obvious beneficiaries of antitrust have been lawyers with an antitrust practice, economists who have collected consulting fees, and, in recent years, business executives and investors whose firms have prevailed in the treble damage suit lottery. A small number of corporate managers, a few thousand at most spread over a century, have had their jobs saved by escaping mergers or market wars that would have occurred in the absence of antitrust. The softening of competition imposed by antitrust has probably transferred some unknown fraction of national income from more efficient, less risk averse, or less scrupulous firms to rivals that were closer to the mean in these qualities. No important piece of antitrust legislation has been passed or retained mainly as a result of political pressures applied by these groups.[2]

During the Great Depression, Congress did pass the Miller-Tydings Act (1937)[3] which legalized a weak (noncollusive) sort of resale price maintenance and the Robinson-Patman Act (1936)[4] which placed some restrictions on seller's power to practice price discrimination. Both laws were supported by lobbying efforts of associations of wholesalers and retailers who were suffering from the aggressive price cutting and sales promotions

---

[2]Many American intellectuals have trouble taking seriously the conjecture of J. M. Keynes that, for the long haul, ideas are more important in shaping economic policy than vested interests (which, when one thinks about it, is a very strange position for intellectuals). In the vested interest tradition, William Baxter has suggested that the political constituency that has kept antitrust going for a century consists of small businessmen who are threatened by changes that increase the scale of efficient production. In his view, antitrust helps them by placing a competitive handicap on their larger rivals.

Baxter was not able to convert his conjecture into a testable hypothesis and I do not find it believable. At any one moment, the number of businessmen so threatened is a tiny fraction of the voting population and a widely scattered and poorly organized one at that. In Washington, their strong suit is the sympathy they inspire, not the cash or votes they can deliver. In any event, antitrust law is mostly judge-made. Federal judges, whatever their faults, are well insulated from the pressures of "the interests." See R. D. Tollison, ed., *The Political Economy of Antitrust: Principal Paper by William Baxter* (1980), pp. 1–57.

[3]50 Stat. 693 (1937).

[4]49 Stat. 1526 (1936).

of larger rivals with lower costs. However, the passage of this legislation occurred more as a result of Congressional desperation induced by the Great Depression than as a result of lobbying by these groups.[5]

The distrust of hard competition apparent in Miller-Tydings and Robinson-Patman had earlier produced the (happily short-lived) codes of the National Industrial Recovery Act[6] that sought price stability through self-government in industry—another name for government sponsored cartels. For a time in the 1930s, many normally sensible people, including even a few economists, were so shaken and confused by the fall in national income that they mistook symptoms for causes. Observing that the depression coincided with falling prices and an eruption of price wars in many markets, they gave their support to legislation intended to raise prices and soften competition.

Admittedly, the influence of pressure groups can be traced in the selection of cases for prosecution by the Justice Department and the Federal Trade Commission. However, an economic rent created by the decision of a single case has an insecure foundation since business practices have substitutes and most have close substitutes. While antitrust is increasingly damned as a source of inefficiency in the American economy, it is, for good reason, almost never cited as a source of economic rents.

Is not antitrust special interest legislation, in the sense of being "pro-consumer"? We shall presently see that antitrust has very likely reduced consumer welfare—at least, as economists understand the term. But again, whatever its impact on consumers, the historical record does not show the hand of self-proclaimed consumer groups in the passage of the basic antitrust statutes—Sherman (1890), Clayton (1914),[7] Federal Trade Com-

---

[5]Many writers have made much of the fact that the counsel for the Wholesale Grocers Association had a hand in the preparation of the bill that became the Robinson-Patman Act, and the record does indicate that several of its provisions were designed to penalize the country's then largest grocery chain (A&P). Benjamin Werne, ed., *Business and the Robinson Patman Law: A Symposium* (1938), pp. 102–4. But, in 1936, the view of many members of Congress that quantity discounts, especially when given secretly, were anticompetitive was already of long standing and had produced the antidiscrimination provisions of the Clayton Act in 1914 (subsequently rendered null by judicial hostility and the small budgets of the Federal Trade Commission). With the shocking mortality rates among small businesses in the Depression, the view gained even more support in Congress. The Robinson-Patman Act may be an affront to economic literacy and legal writing. (It is.) Still, I know of no reason to believe that the Honorable Wright Patman and his followers were not enthusiastically voting their convictions. A long career of discomforting the *Wall Street Journal* would seem to put Patman's populist credentials beyond question.

[6]48 Stat. 195 (1933).

[7]38 Stat. 730 (1914).

mission (1914),[8] and Celler (1950).[9] Clayton is included out of respect for tradition; its practical effects were few and unimportant except as its unfriendly reception in court crystallized Congressional support for more effective measures.

In the Beginning

THE ORIGINS of antitrust have been competently studied at great length and need only be briefly noted here.[10] After the Civil War, a number of new developments in business organization disturbed many politically influential people. Most of these developments, one way or another, were associated with the appearance of business firms larger than the country had known before—though, by present-day measures, the new firms were quite small. The fears engendered by the rise of larger firms produced much hostile, if largely ineffective, legislation at the state level. In 1887, legislation reached the federal level with the Interstate Commerce Commission Act directed at the railroads.[11] Three years later, the fears produced the much more general Sherman Act. In the debates on the trust bills in Congress in 1890, the Standard Oil Company is often denounced. However, it is clear that to the legislators Standard Oil was not a large bureaucratized corporation with "perpetual life" but merely a convenient legal instrument of John D. Rockefeller and a few cronies.

A close reading of the debates and committee hearings that preceeded passage of the Sherman Act can convey a good idea of the specters that inspired it. The Congress of 1890 was troubled by quite a few—the spread of cartels, the plight, real or imagined, of western farmers, shipper grievances over railroad rates, so-called destructive competition, the size of eastern banks, and, above all, the activities of the Standard Oil Company. But the debates and committee hearings do not indicate that Congress in 1890 meant to lay out any detailed agenda for dealing with these concerns. The most that we can infer is that Congress wanted some sort of action from the Attorney General and the courts.

---

[8]38 Stat. 717 (1914).
[9]64 Stat. 1125 (1950).
[10]Notably O. W. Knauth, *The Policy of the United States Toward Industrial Monopoly* (1914), pp. 13–42, H. B. Thorelli, *The Federal Antitrust Policy* (1954), and William Letwin, *Law and Economic Policy in America* (1965).
[11]24 Stat. 379 (1887).

The Machinery

IN RETROSPECT, the Congress of 1890 built far better than anyone of that day seems to have expected or had any right to expect. Some observers cite the fact that the law was passed with only one dissenting vote as evidence that it was not meant to be taken seriously but was merely a Congressional denunciation of sin akin to annual resolutions calling on the Soviet Union to free all captive nations. Such cynicism goes too far. From the hearings and debates, it is clear that the law was carefully drafted in order to minimize the risk that it would be declared unconstitutional by the courts; hence the determination to base the new law on the commerce clause of the Constitution. Given the temper of the Supreme Court in the 1890s, any mention in an antitrust statute of manufacturing, labor, or even corporations, would almost certainly have been voided as an unconstitutional invasion of states' rights.[12]

The Sherman Act's general condemnation of restraint of trade and monopolizing in sections 1 and 2 has stood unchanged for a century. The language of the enforcement provisions authorizes the federal government to seek civil remedies and criminal penalties and provides for private remedies including treble damages and, lest we forget, a reasonable attorney's fee. The antitrust effort was ostensibly reinforced and clarified in 1914 by the Clayton Act and the Federal Trade Commission Act that created the Commission and gave it overlapping jurisdiction with the Justice Department. This wasteful duplication grew out of the rivalry of Congressional committees.[13] Vying for the credit of amending Sherman, the Judiciary Committees reported the Clayton Act and the Interstate Commerce Committees countered with the FTC Act. But both, especially Clayton, were poorly drafted.[14] After the courts had finished with them, they neither

---

[12]For a contemporary assessment of the extent of federal power under the Commerce Clause when the Sherman Act was passed, see A. H. Wintersteen, "The Commerce Clause and the State," 28 (n.s.) *Am. L. Reg.* 733 (1889).

In the 1890s, Congressional fear of the federal courts was well founded, since—at that time—they favored a narrow definition of interstate commerce and federal jurisdiction under the Commerce Clause. The courts had often ruled that "manufacturing is not commerce" and that interstate commerce begins only when goods are delivered to a common carrier for their "final journey" but ends as soon the "original package" in which they are shipped is broken.

[13]J. D. Clark, *The Federal Trust Policy* (1931), pp. 166–68.

[14]For example, supporters of the Clayton Act claimed that it would increase the power of the federal government to block mergers that might get by under a Sherman Act test. But because of careless drafting, Clayton spoke only of mergers effected by the purchase of stock. The merger provision became a dead letter when the Supreme Court held that it could be

added nor subtracted much from what could be done under Sherman. The elegant law of 1890 (it still reads wonderfully well, a century later) has always been the foundation of antitrust, providing the courts with a broad and powerful mandate to devise rules, remedies, doctrines (and myths), for unmapped territory.

A Sketch of Enforcement

THE HISTORY of antitrust enforcement can usefully, if arbitrarily, be divided into five eras. In the years 1890–1905, the enforcement effort was on so slight a scale that its immediate effects on the American economy can only have been negligible. However, litigation in this period did establish two principles that were to have future consequences.

In *Addyston Pipe & Steel Co. v. United States* (1899),[15] the Sherman Act was construed to mean that a cartel agreement to divide markets or fix prices was, for all practical purposes, illegal per se. An unambiguous declaration of the per se rule against price-fixing did not come until 1940;[16] still, after *Addyston Pipe,* the federal courts routinely treated cartels as unlawful conspiracy and refused to credit arguments that sought to justify them on equity or efficiency grounds. In *Northern Securities Co. v. United States* (1904),[17] the federal government obtained the power of corporate divestiture—trust busting in the literal sense—thanks to the unremarkable phrase in the Sherman Act that authorizes the Attorney General to seek enforcement through proceedings in equity. For two hundred years or more before *Northern Securities,* the principal equitable remedy in Anglo-American law had been the simple and uncomplicated injunction.

Neither of the above two cases conferred any discernable benefit on consumers. The three leading firms in the cartel outlawed in the Addyston Pipe case promptly merged without hindrance to form the United Pipe & Foundry Company. The Northern Securities decision merely prevented J. P. Morgan and James Hill from using the convenience of a holding company to vest oversight of three railroads that they already controlled. The rates of these railroads were, in any event, subject to regulation by the Interstate Commerce Commission.

In the second phase, 1906–1920, the antitrust effort achieved its most spectacular results with divestiture decrees entered against the Standard Oil

---

avoided by the simple expedient of acquiring the physical assets of a target company rather than its stock. *Thatcher Manufacturing Co. v. Federal Trade Commission,* 272 U.S. 554 (1926).

[15] *Addyston Pipe & Steel Co. v. United States,* 175 U.S. 211 (1899).

[16] *United States v. Socony-Vacuum Oil Co.,* 310 U.S. 150 (1940).

[17] *Northern Securities Co. v. United States,* 193 U.S. 197 (1904).

Company,[18] the American Tobacco Company,[19] the Corn Products Refining Company,[20] Du Pont,[21] and the country's five largest meatpackers. This phase ended with the failure of the government's nine-year dissolution suit against the United State Steel Corporation in 1920.[22] The steel firm prevailed mainly because the Court was satisfied that it had been a less aggressive and less successful competitor than the Rockefeller, Duke, and Du Pont firms of earlier years. In 1920, the meatpackers, with enemies among the farm lobby in Congress and unfriendly legislation as a possibility, accepted a consent decree that forced their withdrawal from the wholesale grocery trade. The meatpackers broke off the contest despite having, what was for that time, a strong legal position.[23]

The second phase of antitrust enforcement also saw the start of a long and frustrating effort to clarify the status of labor unions under the Sherman Act. Before *Lawlor v. Loewe (Danbury Hatters)* in 1908,[24] there was virtually no body of federal law touching labor unions, their activities being left to common law and state statutes administered by state courts. In any except the most ruthless police states, labor unions have presented difficult and, so far, insoluable problems. They cannot be suppressed, yet—to be effective—they must regularly challenge the State's "monopoly on the legitimate use of violence." The nineteenth-century English judge who doubted that a strike could be both effective and lawful was close to the truth.[25] In a labor dispute, black letter law has always worked to the advantage of the employer who wishes to continue production.

No legal system of a political democracy has yet succeeded in developing deterrents and remedies adequate to deal with strike violence and secondary boycotts. Most of the time none has felt any great need for them, the usual practice being to keep illegalities within reasonable bounds by unwritten ground rules. (The automobiles of nonstrikers may be trashed, but not their homes, etc.)

For better or worse, the Supreme Court in its second attention to *Danbury Hatters* (1915)[26] held that individual members of a labor union whose

---

[18] *Standard Oil Co. of New Jersey v. United States,* 221 U.S. 1 (1911).

[19] *United States v. American Tobacco Co.,* 221 U.S. 106 (1911).

[21] *United States v. E. I. DuPont de Nemours & Co.,* 188 Fed 127 (C.C.D.Del. 1911).

[22] *United States v. United States Steel Corp.,* 251 U.S. 417 (1920).

[23] G. O. Virtue, "The Meat Packing Investigation," 34 Q. J. Econ. 626 (1920). The unsuccessful efforts of the meatpackers to get the restrictive consent decree modified can be traced in *Swift & Co. v. United States,* 276 U.S. 311 (1928), 286 U.S. 106 (1932).

[24] *Lawlor v. Loewe,* 208 U.S. 274 (1908).

[25] See the interruption of counsel by Lord Justice Lindley in *J. Lyons & Sons v. Wilkins,* 1 Ch. 811, 820 (1896).

[26] *Lawlor v. Loewe,* 235 U.S. 522 (1915).

officers, in a contract dispute, knowingly instigated a nationwide second-ary boycott against an employer and all who sold his products were liable for damages (trebled under Sherman) suffered by him. The placing of li-ability on individual union members proved to be intensely unpopular and was soon abandoned by the courts under the prod of the Clayton Act's ringing, if quite erroneous, declaration that "the labor of a human being is not a commodity or article of commerce." Over the next thirty years virtually all "normal" activities of labor unions gained exemption from antitrust;[27] however, the type of boycott condemned in *Danbury Hatters* soon reappeared as an unfair labor practice under the Taft-Hartley Act in 1947.[28]

Whether the courts should ever have applied the generalities of the Sher-man Act to the activities of labor unions depends upon the degree and type of judicial activism one favors. A national policy toward labor unions was inevitable (at least, every developed country has one), and the labor cases decided under Sherman did serve to clarify the issues and reveal what was politically feasible. The function had to be performed by some statute.

Nothing much happened in the third phase of antitrust, 1920–1938. The precedents set in the first two periods seemed to suggest that a "good" trust with less than a 50 percent market share was untouchable; and the most vulnerable corporate targets in the economy had already been at-tacked. Not that the administrations of Harding, Coolidge, and Hoover showed any enthusiasm for making new antitrust law. The Great Depres-sion produced, in the first year of the Roosevelt administration, the loss of economic sanity reflected in the National Industrial Recovery Act and, with it, a virtual repudiation of the assumptions underlying both antitrust and laissez-faire. Fortunately, the loss of sanity was short-lived. Restora-

---

[27]The antitrust liability of labor unions was very largely removed from labor unions by two decisions:

In *Coronado Coal Co. v. United Mine Workers*, 268 U.S. 295 (1925), the Court held that union pressure to raise wages through a strike was lawful provided that the union (1) did not intend to affect the price of the final product and (2), whatever its intent, did not have the power to do so. To take advantage of this doctrine, the union need only show that it regards marketing the product entirely as a management decision.

In *United States v. Hutcheson*, 312 U.S. 219 (1941), the Court, in a decision that was no model of clarity, held that *Danbury Hatters* had been implicitly overruled by subsequent leg-islation, principally the Norris-La Guardia Act, 47 Stat. 70 (1932). Therefore, antitrust no longer applied to secondary boycotts. Since *Hutcheson*, labor unions have only occasionally run afoul of the Sherman Act. This has usually happened when they were cooperating with employers for mutual advantage at the expense of nonunion workers and an employer's competitors.

[28]61 Stat. 136 (1947).

tion was hastened by the decision in *Schechter Poultry Corp v. United States*[29] that the Act was an unconstitutional delegation of legislative power, the unpopularity of many NRA codes, and a limited recovery from the nadir of the depression.

Antitrust policy received its modern cast in the years 1938–1980, during which the domain of Sherman steadily expanded. When antitrust was recalled to life after the demise of the NRA, the rebirth brought a quantum jump in enforcement efforts. In the years 1930–39, the Justice Department fought 85 cases to conclusion, winning 78. In the years 1940–49, notwithstanding World War II, it concluded 382 cases winning 304. The return of the Federal Trade Commission started a little earlier with the number of orders rising from 36 in 1930–1934 to 139 in 1935–1939.[30]

No doubt, a number of chance circumstances played a part in the return of antitrust to favor. There was the flamboyant personality of Thurman Arnold who took over the Antitrust Division in September, 1938. There was the need felt by President Roosevelt and his advisors to be seen to be acting against "economic privilege" without unduly scaring businessmen. Their cooperation was thought necessary for achieving recovery.[31] But the basic "cause" of the revival was a meeting of minds between the hundreds of young economists and lawyers who entered federal service after 1933 and the populist Senators and Congressmen whose power rose with the Democratic majorities during the New Deal. It was, so to speak, a case of Frank Albert Fetter and Louis Brandeis meeting Wright Patman and finding out how much they had in common.

In the two decades following World War II, the Justice Department brought over two dozen divestiture suits which, had they met with total success, would have greatly reduced industry concentration ratios throughout the American economy. In retrospect, this campaign—conducted under the banner of the "new" Sherman Act—seems rather quixotic, since the antitrust agencies had nothing like the resources needed to fight on all of its chosen fronts. The result was mainly "legal victory, economic defeat." Government success made legally suspect not only horizontal mergers but vertical and conglomerate mergers as well. It also raised doubts about concentrated market structures, aggressive pricing to protect or increase market share, intra-industry exchange of price and output information, tying contracts, and exclusive dealing. Nevertheless, judges were more cautious in their decrees than in the language of their opinions.

[29] 295 U.S. 495 (1935).
[30] *The Political Economy of Antitrust,* pp. 24–25.
[31] E. W. Hawley, *The New Deal and the Problem of Monopoly* (1966).

In this postwar period, the government won no dissolution or divestiture victories comparable to the 1911 decrees against the Standard Oil and American Tobacco companies. The most radical surgery was performed on the five major Hollywood producers who, in 1948, were compelled to separate from all of the movie houses that they owned outright or in partnership with exhibitors.[32] The decree removed approximately 2,600 houses from their control. Many were soon closed by the advent of television.

Following World War II, the private remedies provided by the Sherman Act—treble damages and injunctions—for the first time became more than near dead letters. From 1890 to 1940 private damage suits had been successful in only thirteen reported cases.[33] Also for the first time, class actions seeking damages for antitrust violations began to be brought and won. In short, in the years 1938–1980, antitrust became a significant source of income for lawyers and a body of law that had to be taken into account by businessmen in their everyday operations.

The last phase of antitrust began with installation of the Reagan Administration in January 1981 and may, or may not, be over by the time this book goes to press. What Richard Posner calls the "lens of price theory"[34] was applied as never before to antitrust issues by government lawyers and economists. As a result, the government side of antitrust effort was cut back to the harassment of price-fixing agreements and the filing of objections to a few horizontal mergers that perceptibly increased four-firm concentration ratios. A government effort to have the courts rescind the rule that a manufacturer cannot attempt to enforce the price at which his product may be sold by wholesaler or retailer was blocked by Congress.[35]

The Reagan era also saw an increasing reluctance on the part of the courts to award treble damages in private suits. A forty-year rise in private litigation was abruptly reversed and the number of private antitrust suits pending in federal district courts on June 30th declined from 2,423 in 1982 to 1,570 in 1986.[36]

[32] *United States v. Paramount Pictures,* 334 U.S. 131 (1948).
[33] W. J. Donovan and R. R. Irvine, "Proof of Damages Under the Anti-trust Law," 88 *U. Pa. L. Rev.* 511, 525 (1940).
[34] R. A. Posner, "The Chicago School of Antitrust Analysis," 127 (4) *U. Pa. L. Rev.* 925 (1979).
[35] In *Monsanto Co. v. Spray-Rite Corp.,* 465 U.S. 752 (1984), the Justice Department filed a brief supporting Monsanto's program of resale price maintenance enforced by cutting off supplies to distributors who ignored its recommended retail prices. Congress responded by attaching a rider to the appropriation bill of the Justice Department for fiscal 1984, forbidding any funds to be used to argue against the rule that resale maintenance is illegal per se.
[36] *Annual Report of the Director of the Administrative Office of the United States Courts,* 1986, p. 115.

Ironically, these years also saw the consent decree in 1982 that broke up the national Bell telephone system—the most far-reaching and only really disruptive piece of trust-busting ever carried out. In fact, in the whole history of antitrust, the Bell breakup was the only divestiture that had immediate and measurable consequences for consumers and workers.[37]

The Hard Questions

THE LITERATURE on antitrust in the United States is enormous. Even so, two questions have received astoundingly little attention. What economic benefits has the policy conferred and at what costs? How have its benefits and costs been distributed? There is no mystery about the reasons for the neglect of these questions. They cannot be studied without facing up to extremely difficult issues of methodology, theory, and measurement. For most of the years since 1890, economists have not had the data, research budgets, or tools that would permit cost/benefit questions about antitrust to be answered with anything but vague generalities. Indeed, a great part—maybe even the greater part—of what is now called microeconomic theory has been developed in an attempt to throw light on problems forced on the profession's attention by the antitrust experiment.

Also, in politics ambiguity has its uses. Much of the time, it is absolutely essential if conflicts are to be kept within reasonable bounds. So long as the economic consequences of antitrust are only vaguely known, everyone feels free to retain the opinions that he or she has already acquired.

Nobody has ever maintained that real world antitrust is ideal. Its friends have always wanted more and tougher restrictions on freedom on contract and bigger budgets for enforcement. (Forty years ago, a common lament was that "antitrust has never been tried.") Its harshest critics denounce most antitrust rules as welfare-reducing. But the question of tradeoffs is almost never directly addressed. Robert Bork's treatment of costs and benefits in his influential and otherwise incisive book, *The Antitrust Paradox: A Policy at War with Itself* (1978), illustrates the silence on the issue. By Bork's reading, most of antitrust is held to be welfare reducing; however, the rule that price-fixing agreements are illegal per se is held to have conferred enormous benefits on consumers.[38] Bork offers no estimate as to whether the good of the per se rule against price-fixing exceeds the bad of (almost) everything else that he sees in the policy.

---

[37] *United States v. Western Electric Co. Inc., and American Telephone and Telegraph Co.*, 1982–2 Trade Cases, 72, 555.

[38] Robert Bork, *The Antitrust Paradox: A Policy at War with Itself* (1978), p. 263.

A Definition

IN THE interest of brevity, we shall speak throughout this chapter of "antitrust." Since what has been done in the name of the Sherman Act and its children has continually changed over the years, it seems best to indicate the distinctive and enduring features of the policy. In the beginning, antitrust was a Congressional assertion of the power of the federal government. In operation, this power has been used to impose restrictions on freedom of contract not found in the nineteenth century in the common law of the states. Two of these restrictions are important above all others. First, price-fixing agreements are subject to prosecution as criminal offenses. Second, antitrust has softened real world competition to some, largely unknown, extent; this it has done by limiting the kind of injuries that businessmen may inflict upon one another in pursuit of their own interests. In addition, the antitrust agencies have gained the power, subject to court review, to dissolve contractual arrangements that have produced, or may produce, in certain markets levels of ownership concentration that they believe to be undesirable.

In short, the distinctive and enduring features that define antitrust are four: the outlawing of cartels, a (constantly changing) law of unfair competition, controls on mergers, and the occasional breakup or restructuring of established firms—trust-busting in the literal sense. Let us be clear that antitrust is to be defined in terms of its consequences, not in terms of the goals imputed to it. The "suppression of monopoly" or "protection of competition" is often cited an a goal of antitrust but, as we shall see, there are good reasons for believing that antitrust has done little, if anything, to bring about this result. One must, of course, always be on guard against the danger of being taken in by semantic gamesmanship, that is, of accepting that whatever is done in the name of enforcing the antitrust laws is, by definition, an effort to suppress monopoly or protect competition.

Like most things, antitrust is only good or bad in relation to the alternatives. We shall follow common practice and limit comparison to a version of laissez-faire in which the four features cited above have no place. (In chapter 8, we shall consider antitrust in relation to two other possible legal frameworks—ideally regulated monopoly with marginal cost pricing and completely unregulated monopoly.) This version of laissez-faire was, in fact, closely approximated by American business law before 1890 and British business law before the Restrictive Trade Practices Act of 1956.[39] For all practical purposes, cartel agreements were not then treated as crimes

---

[39] 4 & 5 Eliz. 2, c. 68 (1956).

or torts and were sometimes even enforceable in court. The only control on mergers was that provided by the terms of corporate charters. What today are called predatory tactics were legal so long as they did not involve common law crimes or torts and were motivated by disinterested malevolence, that is, simple profit-increasing greed as opposed to irrational, profit-sacrificing, malice.[40]

The Economic Case for Antitrust

ECONOMISTS WHO support antitrust believe that there is a coherent economic theory behind it that is validated by empirical evidence. The theory is quite simple. Other things being equal, the ability of an industry to collect an economic rent from consumers or suppliers increases as its concentration ratio increases or as its member firms act in concert through a cartel to coordinate production and investment. Other things being equal, economic rents are more likely to emerge when competition is "hard," that is, when there are a few restrictions on the competitive tactics that a firm may use to advance its interests. The assumption underlying this simple theory is that a laissez-faire legal environment of the kind that prevailed in the United States in 1890 makes possible the erection of entry barriers that create economic rents—and that this activity can be discouraged by antitrust. Of course, it is possible, though not easy, to favor antitrust, while completely disbelieving this strictly economic case for it.

Economists teach that monopoly reduces economic welfare because it misallocates resources. Misallocation occurs because too little of the monopolized commodity is produced and/or the commodity is produced in a technically inefficient manner. Elimination of the monopoly will bring about a shift of resources which, in principle, will allow people who benefit from the reallocation to compensate people who lose from it and still be better off themselves. Provided that compensation is paid, everyone will be better off in the sense of preferring this new situation to the old. The compensation test is, of course, purely hypothetical. It is never seriously proposed that compensation actually be paid. The only exceptions are cases in which the State has moved to terminate the franchise of a private owner to operate a public utility (toll bridge, ferry, waterworks, etc.).

Identified in this way, the "evil" of monopoly seems clear enough: it makes the nation poorer. But how does one locate and measure a misal-

---

[40]The common law doctrine of disinterested malevolence is most fully elaborated in the English case, *Mogul Steamship Co. v. McGregor, Gow & Co.*, (1892) A.C. 25.

location of resources due to monopoly? A suboptimal allocation is visible to the naked eye only when there exists an entry barrier that creates a capitalized economic rent. In the case of a business firm, this means when the market value of its stocks and bonds clearly and regularly exceeds the replacement value of its physical assets. When this difference is multiplied by an appropriate rate of interest, we have the capital market's estimate of the economic rent accruing to the firm because of its monopoly power.

The economic rent collected by a monopolist is not a welfare loss but only a transfer of income from consumers; the "deadweight" welfare loss imposed by monopoly is the amount of consumer surplus which vanishes, so to speak, into thin air as output is restricted.[41] Various definitions of consumer surplus are in circulation. The most common textbook definition, adequate for our purposes, makes it the difference between what consumers actually pay to obtain a product and what they would have to pay if its production were in the hands of a monopolist who could practice perfect price discrimination, i.e., who could isolate every customer and deal with him on a "take it or leave it" basis.

As a practical matter, estimating deadweight welfare loss is a difficult business.[42] The economic rent of monopoly, when it can be reckoned from

[41]The hard-and-fast distinction between monopoly rent and welfare loss has occasionally been questioned. See, for example, R. A. Posner, "The Social Costs of Monopoly and Regulation," 83 *J. Pol. Econ.* 807 (1975).

The argument is that some part of monopoly rent is also welfare loss because, if monopoly power can be created by investing resources, such a socially wasteful investment will be made. The argument has a certain plausibility when monopoly power depends upon the good will of the State. In the case of regulated public utilities, we observe conspicuous, often lavish, outlays on lobbying, legal harassment of potential competitors, and public relations. But the argument is not relevant to the part of the economy that is subject to antitrust.

It is sometimes asserted, though more often only intimated, that in this unregulated private sector, monopoly power is created and protected by socially wasteful advertising and product differentiation. The fundamental assumptions of price theory permit no such value (I am tempted to write paternalistic) judgment.

When consumers substitute advertised and differentiated varieties for an unadvertised, homogenous commodity, the price theorist must conclude that consumer welfare is increased. To conclude otherwise is to deny that the consumer is competent to spend his income. For good reason, it is often necessary to protect the consumer from himself. Price theory has its limitations as a moral canon. But such protection involves the substitution of politics for markets and raises issues beyond the scope of this book.

[42]The first effort at estimating welfare loss from monopoly in the private unregulated sector of the economy was made by Arnold Harberger for all American manufacturing industries for the period 1924–28. By his result, the loss was trivial—"less than a tenth of a percent of the national income." "Monopoly and Resource Allocation," 44 *Am. Econ. Rev.* 77, 86 (May 1954).

Subsequent studies for later years have produced somewhat higher figures for welfare loss but not high enough to indicate that in the private unregulated sector it is a problem worth

the difference between a firm's market value and the value of its physical assets, is the best proxy for welfare loss that has yet been found. The greater the economic rent created by monopoly, the greater the welfare loss imposed on the economy. However, when the firm's demand curve is "normal"—when its marginal revenue declines more rapidly than price as output increases, as in the diagrams of economic textbooks—welfare loss is always less than monopoly rent. Unfortunately, capitalized rents are highly visible and easily measured only in government-regulated industries with strictly enforced entry barriers.

In the city of New York, a totally demolished legal (yellow) taxicab has a market value exceeding $100,000. (We assume that the wreck still has attached the medallion that makes it a legal taxicab.) If we take 10 percent per annum as the interest rate for discount purposes, this indicates that a taxicab owner is collecting a rent of at least $10,000 a year from his riders. This monstrosity is possible because the number of permits to operate taxicabs has been fixed by law for over sixty years; and because the police department invests scarce resources to harass the thousands of illegal taxicabs that ride the streets in order to preserve the most lucrative sectors of the city for legal taxicabs, notably mid-Manhattan and the airports. Likewise, the discrepancy between the market value of a big city television station and the modest replacement value of its studio and transmitter has an obvious explanation—a government-imposed limit on the number of permits to operate television stations.

In the unregulated, private sector of the economy—the domain of antitrust—capitalized economic rents are hardly ever "obvious" but must be painstakingly sought in messy accounting data. In the case of large firms, there is the added complication that a highly volatile securities market makes it difficult to estimate the market value of the firm in order to calculate economic rent. Therefore, an alternative technique for locating and measuring rent is favored by most investigators. An attempt is made to measure the rate of return on equity capital employed in the firm over a number of years. From the figure derived, some average rate of return on equity capital for the economy is subtracted and the difference is treated as a monopoly rent.

---

worrying about. Most put loss in the neighborhood of one percent. See, for example, D. A. Worcester, "New Estimates of the Welfare Loss to Monopoly, 1956–1969," 40 *So. Econ. J.* 234 (1973).

One later study did raise the welfare loss at between 4 and 13 percent of "gross corporate product." But it did so by the culturally presumptuous expedient of treating advertising outlays as "waste." The study was based on data for 734 firms for the period 1963–66. Keith Cowling and D. C. Mueller, "The Social Costs of Monopoly Power," 88 *Econ. J.* 727 (1978).

Most studies, of which there are now a very great number, have found that highly concentrated industries tend to have rates of return on equity capital from 10 to 20 percent above the average rate of return used for comparison. (The difference is, of course, less when the comparison is made for rates of return on total capital employed.) One study has found that, in manufacturing, the highest rates of return are found in industries where the largest firm has a market share exceeding 40 percent.[43] As yet, the economic meaning of the difference in reported rates of return between high and low concentration industries is not clear. A monopoly explanation is not the only game in town.[44]

Some investigators hold that the difference in profitability between high and low concentration industries disappears after allowance is made for the fact that the higher returns are associated with higher risk.[45] George Stigler once disposed of this difference in manufacturing industries with a deft statistical correction. He noted that low concentration industries have a greater percentage of small firms and then assumed that they are better at shielding income from taxation by expensing profits (relatives on the payroll, etc.). After an allowance was made for this small firm advantage, high concentration and low concentration industries were found to have the same rates of return on total capital.[46]

Then too, as we shall see in chapter 5, when there is free entry into a market that can support only a few firms, the presumption derived from price theory is that more concentrated industries will tend to have higher rates of return than low concentration industries; and the explanation of this association is simply the inevitability of fixed cost in the firm, not monopoly power based on an entry barrier. For there are markets in which n sellers earn above average rates of return when n + 1 sellers would incur losses. This truth is well known to merchants in small towns.

So far as decisions about policy are concerned, does it really matter which interpretation of the data on profitability is correct? I doubt it. Any economic rents due to monopoly that exist in the unregulated private sector of the economy are so small that there can be no presumption that antitrust action to remove them would be cost effective. By way of contrast, in the regulated private sector this presumption is easily satisfied. With no great effort, there we can find long term rates of return on equity capital in

[43] W. G. Shepherd, "The Elements of Market Structure," 54 *Rev. Econ. Stat.* 25 (1972).

[44] For a sophisticated exploration of the problems involved in explaining the association between concentration ratios in industry and profit rates, see Harold Demsetz, "Economics as a Guide to Antitrust Regulation," 19 *J. Law Econ.* 371 (1976).

[45] W. G. Shepherd, *The Economics of Industrial Organization,* 2d ed. (1985), 130–32.

[46] G. J. Stigler, *Capital and Its Rates of Return in Manufacturing Industries* (1963).

excess of 50 percent per annum. In the (legal) taxicab industry of New York City, the rate of return for three decades has been in the neighborhood of a scarcely believable 200 percent per annum.[47] For a time in the 1970s, a permit to operate a taxicab in the city sold for more than a seat on the New York Stock Exchange.

What of the profitability of price-fixing agreements which in the United States are generally termed "conspiracies," since they are illegal unless expressly exempted from the Sherman Act? The participants prosecuted by the antitrust agencies may be guilty of acting together to achieve common goals but the evidence indicates that their efforts are not rewarded with economic rents. We have two large sample studies of manufacturing firms prosecuted for cartel membership. One found that they actually earned a rate of return on equity capital below that of comparable firms never prosecuted.[48] The other found that they managed to earn an average rate of return.[49] These results are not really surprising. Being illegal, the conspiracies in question were furtive, loosely organized, and naked to the competition of nonmembers. To anticipate, the thesis of chapter 6 is that, when there is no barrier to entry, the raison d'être of a cartel is the reduction of uncertainty for its members, not the creation of an economic rent.

Economic rents traceable to monopoly are always associated with resource misallocation and hence with welfare loss. But it is at least conceivable that monopoly—in the limited sense of power to influence price—can impose a welfare loss without creating a rent. To meet this difficulty, it is sometimes urged that the Lerner index should be used to measure "monopoly power."[50] The (Abba) Lerner index is the difference of price and marginal cost divided by price. The assumption of writers who favor this index is that economic welfare would be increased if, somehow, price could be made equal to marginal cost.

---

[47]Let us make the reality-based assumptions that (1) the market value of a permit (medallion) to share in the New York taxicab monopoly is $100,000, (2) the future earnings of a taxicab are discounted at a rate of 10 percent per annum, and (3) the amount of "real" capital needed to keep a taxicab on the streets is $5,000—$4,000 invested in a used hack plus $1,000 in garage space and support equipment. The $100,000 needed to buy the permit to participate in the monopoly is, of course, no part of real capital.

The monopoly rent earned by operating the taxicab is $100,000 × .10 or $10,000 per annum. The monopoly rate of return on the capital employed is $10,000/$5,000 or 200 percent.

[48]Peter Asch and J. J. Seneca, "Characteristics of Collusive Firms," 23 *J. Ind. Econ.* 223 (1975), and "Is Collusion Profitable?," 58 *Rev. Econ. Stat.* 58 (1976).

[49]Dosung Choi and G. C. Phillippatos. "Financial Consequences of Antitrust Enforcement," 65 *Rev. Econ. Stat.* 50 (1983).

[50]W. M. Landes and R. A. Posner, "Market Power in Antitrust Cases," 94 *Harv. L. Rev.* 937 (1981).

A minor objection to the Lerner index as a monopoly measure is that since marginal cost is not an accounting category, some proxy must be found for it. The major objection to the Lerner index is that it is really a measure of aggregated market imperfections and includes, for example, those due to transportation costs. Most such imperfections are imposed by Nature; therefore, there can be no presumption that, except in an economic model in which imperfections are assumed away, policies that would make price equal to some proxy for marginal cost would increase economic welfare. It is difficult enough to estimate the welfare loss of monopoly associated with rents. At present, we have no way of estimating the welfare loss of monopoly (assuming that it exists) that does not produce an economic rent.

Price Theory and Antitrust

CAN "CONVENTIONAL" price theory—the kind now taught in virtually all the universities of the world outside the most repressive Marxist states—tell us anything about the relative merits of antitrust and laissez-faire as rule sets that affect economic welfare? The answer is yes, but for friends of antitrust it provides no comfort. All modern economic analysis assumes that people ascend to higher indifference curves, and so attain more welfare, by engaging in exchange. However we disguise it in rhetoric, antitrust is a set of restrictions on freedom of contract. Therefore, when viewed through Posner's "lens of price theory," the presumption must be that antitrust is welfare-reducing.

This presumption can only be set aside in one of two ways: by showing that one party to the exchange is too incompetent, ill-informed, or immature to look after his own interests; or by showing that the exchange has malign externalities, that is, welfare-reducing effects for third parties greater than the welfare gain that it secures for the parties directly involved. Thus, as a matter of logic, there can be no general argument derived from price theory that supports antitrust. To justify an antitrust rule, it is necessary first to show that there are "special circumstances" which strongly point to the lack of contractual competence on the part of one party or to the emergence of malign externalities if the State does not intervene.

Let us be clear that the part of price theory which deals with the behavior of a monopolist is irrelevant to the issues raised by the vast majority of cases litigated under the antitrust laws. Monopoly theory assumes the existence of an entry barrier and hence the presence of an economic rent and welfare loss. Thus, by definition, "true" monopoly imposes a malign externality on the economy. But, in the real world, producers who do not enjoy the patronage of the State have no long-run (and little short-run) protection against rivals. There are, of course, a few esoteric exceptions to this proposition, notably monopolies conferred by control of a scarce natural resource (the South African diamond cartel is a favorite textbook example) or monopolies enforced by violence in the underworld. Cases dealing with these exceptions form, at most, a short footnote to the history of antitrust. The seller whose behavior is described by the monopoly theory of the textbooks has no competitors, actual or potential. If actions involving charges of collusion are excepted, the defendant in an antitrust case is invariably in court not because of anything done to injure consumers but because he is alleged to have done something to injure competitors, actual or potential. And, in collusion cases, no actual injury to consumers need be shown in order to establish guilt—only the fact of collusion.

What of that part of price theory that deals with competition among the few—oligopoly in the useful, if inelegant, word popularized by Edward Chamberlin? When sellers are few and protected by an entry barrier, oligopoly is merely "incomplete monopoly" and oligopoly theory is as irrelevant to antitrust problems as monopoly theory. Given an entry barrier and no antitrust rules to worry about, oligopoly is not even a stable form of market organization; the oligopolists can increase their joint profits by merging or forming a cartel. The immense (and unfortunate) popularity of oligopoly theory in American economics is, in fact, a backhanded tribute to the success of antitrust in suppressing cartels and blocking mergers.

When no barrier blocks the entry of new firms, it is to be expected that the number of firms in a market will be determined by the magnitude of consumer demand in relation to the optimum size of the individual firm. As we shall see in chapter 8, a theory of oligopoly that posits free entry has its uses for understanding the determination of price and output. But it can provide no support for antitrust. With free entry, the incomplete collusion of oligopoly leads to excess capacity because firms produce outputs at which unit cost is falling. For this, the dedicated welfare economist's remedy is regulated, efficient, monopoly—the marginal cost pricing of economic theory textbooks. An antitrust intervention that adds additional firms to an industry that already has excess capacity is, on its face, welfare-destroying.

In the light of what has been said above, it is reasonable to ask: why antitrust? No solid evidence exists that monopoly without the protection of the State is, or ever has been, a source of significant welfare loss in the American economy. What has long passed for the economic theory of antitrust is, on its face, implausible, if not downright unbelievable.

Two answers come quickly to mind. One is that antitrust is not really about containing monopoly as a way of increasing economic welfare. Perhaps a different game is being played—as an English visitor concluded after a study of antitrust,[51] and Learned Hand suggested in a famous dicta in *Alcoa*.[52] The other answer is that truths which seem clear enough today were only slowly learned and digested over many years. Explaining the popularity of antitrust is difficult because both answers apply. Still, given the clear contradictions between the premises of price theory and those of the economic case for antitrust, how did virtually the whole of the American economics profession ever come to believe, with a conviction often bordering on religious fervor, that antitrust increases economic welfare? While the question is a fair one, we postpone it for the moment.

The Unimportance of "Original Intent"

ECONOMISTS PROPERLY worry about the effects of antitrust on economic welfare. While this concern does us credit, it does not justify reading a goal of welfare maximization into the Sherman Act as Robert Bork does in *The Antitrust Paradox* (and as as many others have done before him). Bork appears to argue that the policy was intended by Congress to promote welfare by promoting competition; yet it has been subverted by the courts into a policy of reducing welfare by protecting competitors from the consequences of competition.[53] Bork's position is that no antitrust rule

[51] A. D. Neale, *The Antitrust Laws of the United States of America* (1960), especially ch. 15.

On leave from the Board of Trade in London, Neale was quite clear by the end of his study that the main concern of American antitrust was with the dispersion of power, not efficiency. He seems to have had doubts as to whether European countries with per capita incomes at that time well under this country's would be interested in antitrust on the American model.

[52] "It is possible, because of its indirect social or moral effect, to prefer a system of small producers, each dependent for his success upon his own skill and character, to one in which the great mass of those engaged must accept the direction of a few. These considerations, which we have suggested only as possible purposes of the Act, we think the decisions prove to have been in fact its purposes." *United States v. Aluminum Co. of America*, 148 F.2d 416, 428 (2d cir. 1945).

A cynic might point out that, even after the most Draconian imposition of trust busting imaginable, the great majority of us would still be working for somebody else.

[53] Most readers of Bork, myself included, at first believed that the "antitrust paradox" of the book's title conveyed his conviction that the courts have transformed the Sherman act from a protection of competition as a policy of consumer protection into a protection of competitors from the consequences of competition. Bork later claimed that he had meant nothing

is justified unless there is a presumption grounded in price theory that it will increase output.

Economists are entitled to argue that the promotion of economic welfare ought to be the paramount, preferably the only, goal of antitrust.[54] However, the view that Congress intended the primacy of this goal when it passed the Sherman Act in 1890 is historically suspect and can only be supported, if at all, by a highly selective use of evidence. Even if this view were correct, it would be irrelevant to the administration of antitrust after one hundred years of case law.

As we noted earlier, a close reading of the debates and committee hearings that preceded passage of the Sherman Act can convey a good idea of the fears that inspired it but not much else. The members of the Senate Judiciary Committee who drafted the act that received John Sherman's name,[55] did take care to insure that the Supreme Court would not throw it out as an unconstitutional invasion of states rights—hence the wise determination to rest the new law on the Commerce Clause with no mention of manufacturing, labor unions, or other specifics. The debates and hearings do provide some evidence that the new law was intended to outlaw cartels. There seems to have been a consensus that it would make illegal the price-fixing agreements that, by (debatable) Congressional reading, the common law had only treated as unenforceable contracts. However, the Sherman Act is statute, not Constitution. What Congress intended by it in 1890 is now of antiquarian interest only. Every Congress since then has had the opportunity to correct any court decisions that it found objectionable. Changes have been few and far between and have left intact,

---

so naive. Rather, he intended to convey that whatever the Act's original intent, if the courts had practiced good law, they would have placed the most direct and reasonable interpretation on the language of the statute; and that had this been done, it would have served to promote consumer welfare. "Economics and Antitrust: Response," 3 *Contemporary Policy Issues* 35 (1984–85).

[54] The shock and indignation which is triggered when economists discover late in the game that real world antitrust actually has antiefficiency features is sometimes quite touching. Thus:

There is a specter that haunts our antitrust institutions. Its threat is that, far from serving as the bulwark of competition, these institutions will become the most powerful instrument in the hands of those who wish to subvert it. More than that, it threatens to draw great quantities of resources into the struggle to prevent effective competition, thereby more than offsetting the contributions to economic efficiency promised by antitrust activities. W. J. Baumol & J. A. Ordover, "Use of Antitrust to Subvert Competition," 28 *J. Law Econ.* 247 (1985).

[55] The Sherman Act was mainly drafted by Senator George Edmunds of Vermont with help from Senators James George of Mississippi and George Hoar of Massachusetts. The original bill of Senator John Sherman of Ohio had been made unwieldy, and almost certainly unconstitutional, by floor amendments. William Letwin, *Law and Economic Policy in America* (1965), pp 87–95.

except for the periodic revision of penalties, the substantive clauses of the
Sherman Act—the big guns of sections 1 and 2.

The Very Real Achievements of Antitrust

IN TRYING to divine the goals of antitrust, we should, I think, assume
with Justice Holmes that people must be presumed to intend the consequences of their actions. Its goals are to be inferred from its effects, not
from the rhetoric of judges and commentators. We do not know much
about the welfare consequences of antitrust except that, for its first half
century, they must have been small. But there is no doubt about the policy's impact on the corporate structure of the American economy.

Antitrust has prevented the cartelization of the economy. Of this there
can be no reasonable doubt.[56] By placing obstacles in the way of intra-
industry mergers and occasionally busting up firms, it has reduced concentration ratios throughout the economy.[57] Antitrust has also changed the
way business is conducted by softening competition to some largely unknown (and probably unmeasurable) extent. These achievements may have
done nothing for the American consumer. Most likely, they have injured
him. (This verdict is based on the admittedly unprovable and implausible
assumption that, without antitrust, the laissez-faire legal environment of

[56]Occasionally an economist can be found who questions the conclusion that antitrust is necessary to prevent the cartelization of the economy. For the empirically oriented, my proof
is an invitation to cite an economy which has operated during the last hundred years without
antitrust rules that was not (or is not) cartelized. This challenge can be made with confidence.
There are none.

For the theorist, the invitation is to write down the conditions for efficient production in
an industry that is not perfectly competitive. A necessary condition, of course, is that production must be allocated in a way that keeps marginal cost equal in all firms. This condition
cannot be realized without an arrangement that assigns and enforces production quotas and,
if necessary divides profits. In the absence of antitrust, the cartel is a perfectly rational and
inevitable form of business organization.

Cartels are a very mixed bag. Some are little more than luncheon gatherings where the
business outlook is discussed. Others perform most of the functions of a multiplant firm.
The economist's expectation is that, when the Law permits, firms will invest in collusion
("joint income maximization" is a less emotionally laden term) so long as the additional
expected return is greater than the additional cost (chapter 6).

[57]For evidence that antitrust has been mainly responsible for the decline in concentration at
the industry level in the American economy that has occurred over the last half century, see
W. G. Shepherd, "Causes of Increased Competition in the U.S. Economy, 1939–1980," 64
Rev. Econ. Stat. 613 (1982).

Shepherd's title for his article is, I believe, misleading since it is really about changes in
industrial concentration. His unstated premise is, of course, that concentration is a legitimate
proxy for "competition," a view which, for the reasons indicated throughout this book, I
do not accept.

1890 would have remained in place.) But these achievements have been popular enough to make antitrust a sacrosanct symbol in American politics. If the language of the first two sections of the Sherman Act is not a part of the Constitution, it might as well be.

Antitrust and the Populist Impulse

FOR A long time after I began to doubt that antitrust does anything to increase economic welfare, I was puzzled by its immense popularity as an ideal—even among economists. While antitrust may misallocate resources to our dismay, it creates scarcely any of the economic rents that are the most common raison d'être of political constituencies. As noted above, the only obvious beneficiaries of antitrust are members of the antitrust bar, a few economic consultants, a few corporate executives whose jobs were saved by antitrust barriers against mergers, and, in recent decades, managers and stockholders whose firms win treble damage suits.

The popularity of antitrust no longer surprises me. It has come to seem perfectly reasonable in a country that is dedicated to the preservation of bicameral state legislatures (even in Rhode Island), the Electoral College, independent sewer districts, juries in civil cases, township governments, grand juries, and popular election of coroners. Not to overlook state constitutions that specify the width of ski trails in state parks and detail who may receive railroad passes. All of these institutions have two things in common. They are thought to disperse power and they undoubtedly do operate to disperse decision-making. Only rarely does anyone, most likely some sort of college professor, question whether they are worth what they cost in terms of alternatives sacrificed.

College courses in historical methods used to teach (maybe they still do) that "inevitable" is the favorite word of mediocre historians who write history as apology for the victors and have not the wit to imagine what might have been. But surely there was something very nearly inevitable about the appearance of antitrust on the American scene in 1890.

Given the primitive character of the federal civil service at that time, any policy to deal with the concerns of Congress could only have been enforced through the federal courts. Given the novelty and complexity of some of the problems faced, Congress had no choice but to confer broad discretionary power on the courts. This was just as well. In the 1890s, any policy that sought to bypass the judges would have been almost certainly have been declared unconstitutional or nullified by the imposition of crippling due process requirements (as was the fate of the original Interstate Commerce Commission Act). The policy launched by the Sherman Act was cheap, at least in the beginning, and it delivered a quick and visible payoff with the outlawing of cartels in *Addyston Pipe* (1899).[58] An even more dazzling payoff seemed to come when the Supreme Court ordered the breakup of the Standard Oil and American Tobacco companies in 1911.

No significant opposition to antitrust developed as it gained momentum and the original skeptics passed from the scene or were converted. Except for a few socialists and Social Darwinians, very soon (almost) all men came to speak well of it. There was the notable exception of Justice Holmes, though his harshest criticism of antitrust was reserved for private correspondence. "The Sherman Act is a humbug based on economic ignorance and incompetence."[59] Admittedly, nobody could prove that antitrust was doing anything to benefit consumers. But then nobody could prove that it was doing anything to injure them. Finally, as time passed, antitrust gained the presumption in favor of the status quo that, in stable political systems, is usually granted to policies and institutions that offend few.

Doubt and Acceptance

GIVEN THE national bias in favor of decentralized decision-making, I am no longer surprised by the popularity of antitrust. However, I still do find puzzling (and fascinating) the way in which the views of economists on antitrust have developed and changed over the years.

We can pass quickly through the decades. Economists had nothing to do with the passage of the Sherman Act in 1890.[60] It was greeted by our then new and tiny profession with a mixture of indifference, hostility, and contempt. True, Alfred Marshall following the trust controversy from the other side of the Atlantic had kind words for the new law but I do not believe that he understood the American politics that produced it.[61] Young American economists back from their exciting studies in Bismarck's Germany saw it as an impertinent interference with a Zeitgeist that was decreeing ever greater size and centralization. Older economists raised on the British classics saw the Sherman Act as a departure from the wisdom of

---

[58] *Addyston Pipe & Steel Co. v. United States*. 175 U.S. 211 (1899).

[59] Justice Holmes to Sir Frederick Pollock, April 23, 1910. J. J. Marke ed., *The Holmes Reader*, 2d ed. (1964), p. 112.

[60] The intellectual origins of the Sherman act have been exhaustively studied. See, especially, H. B. Thorelli, *The Federal Antitrust Policy* (1954), pp. 108–27, and William Letwin, *Law and Economic Policy in America* (1965), pp. 71–77.

[61] *Report of the Sixteenth Meeting of the British Association for the Advancement of Science* (1891), pp. 898, 905. However, Marshall doubted that, even in the absence of restrictive legislation, many combinations would be able to emulate the success of Standard Oil—"the only Trust which can show a long record of undisputed success on a large scale."

laissez-faire. Since colleges and universities no longer teach much history of economic thought, now it is not widely known that the American Economic Association was founded by young Germanophiles; and that their plainly avowed purpose was to encourage German-style research and give a hearing to critics of laissez-faire. Their bête noire was the social Darwinism of William Graham Sumner and its support of extreme laissez-faire.

Somewhere between 1900 and 1920, majority opinion among American economists swung behind antitrust.[62] The acceptance was rapid and total. If Marxists are excepted, not a single American-trained economist of any prominence questioned the desirability of antitrust in the interwar years, though many doubted its effectiveness. Even refugee scholars from Europe, notably Joseph Schumpeter,[63] Ludwig von Mises,[64] and Herbert von Beckerath,[65] who clearly disbelieved the assumptions underlying antitrust, did not go out of their way to attack it. I suspect that they regarded antitrust as a puzzling but probably unimportant bit of American folly—far below the evil influence of Marx and Keynes.

How and why did this very sudden and abrupt change in opinion come about? An uncharitable judgment would be that it was another case of "if you can't lick them, join them." For, by 1920, it was clear that antitrust was here to stay. There was more to the story than this. Persuaded by theoretical and empirical work that they accepted as "best evidence," economists came to believe that the popular hostility to "big business" had an economic justification.

The turning point in professional opinion is marked by the appearance in 1901 of Charles Bullock's once famous survey of the "trust" literature which found virtually no evidence that the wave of corporate mergers which was then was sweeping the economy could be explained by the need to achieve economies of scale.[66] Bullock was an academic economist of standing (Williams, later Harvard) who had also written a first-rate and widely used introductory textbook. Two years later a leading financial journalist, John Moody, said much the same thing in his widely read *The Truth About the Trusts*. With the appearance of J. B. Clark and J. M. Clark's *The Control of Trusts* (1912), the desirability of antitrust became part of the received

---

[62]A recent study argues that the big change in economists' opinion did not come until the 1920s. T. J. DiLorenzo and Jack High, "Antitrust and Competition, Historically Considered," 26 *Econ. Inquiry* 423 (1988). My dating of the change is, I believe, based upon a larger sample of writings.

[63]Joseph Schumpeter, *Capitalism, Socialism, and Democracy,* 3d ed. (1950).

[64]Ludwig von Mises, *Planning for Freedom,* (1952).

[65]Herbert von Beckerath, *Modern Industrial Organization* (1933).

[66]C. J. Bullock, "Trust Literature: a Survey and a Criticism," 15 *Q. J. Econ.* 167 (1901).

wisdom in American economics.[67] At this time, the elder Clark (J. B.) was the most widely honored economist in the United States. He had never been known to say a good word for populist causes.

George Stigler has suggested that it was the growing acquaintance of American economists with the formal model of perfect competition that caused them to fall in behind antitrust, the implication being that they came to use the model as a standard by which real-world industries were judged.[68] A harsh judgment on our profession if true! (I doubt that Stigler meant it in this way.) Creeping professionalism may have had something to do with the change in opinion. The tendency to confuse a model useful for illuminating reality with reality itself is a permanent occupational hazard in all scientific work, though it is most easily detected in the social sciences.[69] (This confusion has been called the "tyranny of abstraction.") But creeping professionalism does not explain the fervor of the conversion of economists to antitrust. The simpler and more easily documented explanation is that they concluded that large multiplant firms with large market shares had neither an efficiency justification nor any other redeeming virtue. Hence such corporate giants, e.g., John D. Rockefeller's oil com-

[67]This joint effort of father and son was far more supportive of the antitrust effort that an earlier book by J. B. Clark alone, *The Control of Trusts: An Argument in Favor of Curbing the Power of Monopoly by a Natural Method* (1901). "The "natural method" of the elder Clark is little more than laissez-faire purged of "predatory" practices, especially railroad rebates. The change in emphasis was probably due to the influence of the son since, according to the preface of the later book, he did most of the rewriting.

[68]G. J. Stigler, "The Economists and the Problem of Monopoly," 72 *Am. Econ. Rev.* 1 (May 1982).

[69]Economists are regularly reproached, both from inside and outside the profession, with judging the performance of real world industries in terms of how closely they approximate a model of perfect competition. Most of this criticism is directed at straw men and is simply irrelevant. Of course, most people finish their formal training in economics, whether at the freshman or Ph.D. level, with the idea that markets with many sellers are more competitive than those with few sellers. But as anyone who has ever taught an introductory course in economics knows, most people begin their formal training in economics with this belief. Whether it is strengthened or weakened by course work is an empirical question.

Unfortunately, semantics here lifts its ugly head. "Competition" is a term that defies an all-purpose definition. As most people understand the term, real world markets with many sellers *are* more competitive than those with fewer sellers. In low concentration markets, there is typically more choice of product models, more fluctuation in prices, more haggling over prices, and a more rapid turnover of firms.

If economists can be faulted for the way we teach the young, it is because we do not make clear that, so far as economic welfare is concerned, the differences between high and low concentration markets are mostly unimportant. Unless sellers are collecting rents big enough to indicate a welfare loss that it would be cost effective to eliminate by State intervention, such features as price leadership, product differentiation, advertising, administered prices, and even collusion do not matter.

pany, were expendable. This is the way students of my generation were still learning it from Henry Simons at the University of Chicago in the early 1940s.

> Few of our gigantic corporations can be defended on the ground that their present size is necessary to reasonably full exploitation of production economies; their existence is to be explained in terms of opportunities for promoter profits, personal ambitions of industrial and financial "Napoleons," and advantages of monopoly power.[70]

This was the all-important thought that Chicago undergraduates of my day were expected to carry away from their introduction to the modern corporation. The sophomore who spoke up in class soon found that a belief that big firms were big because size made possible scale economies was treated by teaching assistants as a sign of naiveté or something worse. Back east, the view that all significant economies of scale relate to the plant was elevated to a "fundamental principle" by Frank Albert Fetter.[71]

In retrospect, we know that Bullock and all who followed him in doubting the importance of scale economies as a force behind mergers, especially those who did the trust studies for the Bureau of Corporations and the early Federal Trade Commission, "got it wrong." The earlier studies of the United States Industrial Commisssion prepared under the direction of Jerimiah Jenks, a much underrated economist, had been cautiously respectful of scale economies as cause of the merger movement.[72] The students of the "trust problem" in the early years of this century made two mistakes which have been repeated in merger studies ever since. The first was the failure to recognize that the prospect of a cost saving, however, small, is a force making for industrial concentration. Indeed, there is no reason why, over time, very small scale economies should not produce very big changes in measures of concentration. The second mistake was the failure to recognize that the "true" motives behind a merger are ir-

---

[70] H. C. Simons, "A Positive Program for Laissez Faire" in *Economic Policy for a Free Society* (1948), p. 52.

[71] F. A. Fetter, "The Fundamental Principle of Efficiency in Mass Production," in *Relative Efficiency of Large, Medium-Sized, and Small Business* 398 (TNEC Monograph No. 13, 1941).

[72] See, for example, the book that Jenks distilled from his work with the Industrial Commission, *The Trust Problem* (1903).

While Jenks was neither an economic theorist nor a statistician, he was a very careful observer of the business world. Thus he early pointed that, when competition is not perfect, one advantage that the multiplant firm has over a loose cartel is its power to open and close plants in response to changes in demand—a truth still often overlooked in the discussion of scale economies. See his "The Development of the Whiskey Trust," 4 *Political Science Quarterly* 297 (1889).

relevant to the future of the firm that it creates. Even if corporate promoters are driven by unbridled lust for a monopoly rent, a maniacal desire
to head the biggest firm in the universe, or a quick killing in the stock
market, their efforts will not provide a viable enterprise if greater size has
a negative impact upon efficiency. Downsizing and spinoffs are, as we
know, everyday events in the business world.

Admittedly the only economies of scale that can be precisely measured
relate to the plant. Here, all that is needed for a good approximation are
detailed engineering and accounting data. Scale economies "external to the
plant and internal to the firm" is an open-ended category; the same is true
of scale diseconomies. (Quantity discounts on the purchase of paperclips
versus the cost of another copying machine or another vice president).
Both can be cited ad infinitum but only a highly subjective balance can be
struck between them. Of necessity, studies of economies internal to the
firm and external to the plant have been based on the investigator's impres-
sions and interviews with industry people. My reading of the evidence is
that, in most industries most of the time, there are, over a wide range of
output, scale economies external to the plant (and internal to the firm),
but that these economies are "small"; thus most large multiplant firms
operate under conditions of something close to constant long-run unit
cost—as most cost studies seem to show.[73] If it were not so, this country's
ventures in trust-busting would not have been politically possible. Too
many workers would have lost their pensions and too many stockholders,
not excluding widows and orphans, would have suffered capital losses.

The failure of empirical studies to support the thesis that the trust movements before 1914 was motivated mainly by the desire to achieve economies of scale was not the only the reason why antitrust gained popularity
among economists. The work of J. B. Clark and J. M. Clark gave intellectual respectability to the view that predatory competition could be used
to eliminate competitors and erect an entry barrier that could generate an
economic rent.

The work of Arthur Stone Dewing indicating that many of the large

---

[73]For a discussion of the problems involved in conducting a study of cost in a multiplant
firm, see F. M. Scherer et al., *The Economics of Multi-Plant Operation: An International Comparison* (1975).

Scherer and company agree that almost all previous studies, of which there are a great
number, have denied or underestimated scale economies in multiplant firms. Even so, most
such economies found in their study were quite modest and exhausted after a few plants (five
or less) had been brought under common control. Still, as argued above, when the object is
to explain firm size, the magnitude of the scale economy is irrelevant. The usual other things
being equal, firms will grow to take advantage of the cost saving of size no matter how
small.

firms created by merger before 1914 were financial failures was also widely accepted as supporting the case for antitrust though it really did nothing of the kind.[74] The economic success of an enterprise and the financial success of its backers are two different magnitudes. If a firm formed by merger falls into financial receivership, is reorganized, and continues as a going concern, its formation is justified by an efficiency test; subsequent financial failure and reorganization only prove that the promoters had overestimated future earnings. Most of the firms studied by Dewing remained in existence for many years under one name or another. Some are still around.

Depression and Confusion

THE INTEREST of economists in antitrust issues was fueled by the torrent of criticism of the business world that erupted in the Great Depression. Two developments especially troubled the profession. On the one hand, most economists were disturbed, if not appalled, at the flood of crank proposals for dealing with the catastrophy, particularly those calling for national planning to eliminate "destructive competition"—proposals that ultimately produced the short-lived National Industrial Recovery Administration and its promotion of industry-crafted codes of "fair competition."[75] On the other hand, many economists came to feel in their bones that the growth of large firms had somehow produced a "decline of competition" that deepened and prolonged the depression.

Looking back, it is hard to believe that leading American economists of that day really believed with Gardiner Means that the price rigidities that appeared to characterize highly concentrated markets had been a major factor causing or prolonging the depression (compared with the contraction of the money supply between 1929 and 1933).[76] But the record indicates that this is exactly what they did believe. In the spring of 1932, a number of the profession's leaders, fearing that either or both political parties would adopt planks inimical to antitrust, prepared a statement for the national conventions to be held that summer. The statement flatly denied that the Sherman Act had served to create excess capacity or overproduction or had anything to do with the crisis at hand. It then went on the offensive.

---

[74] A. S. Dewing, *Corporate Promotions and Reorganizations* (1914) and "A Statistical Test of the Success of Consolidations," 36 Q. J. Econ., 84 (1921).
[75] 48 Stat. 195 (1933).
[76] G. C. Means, *Industrial Prices and Their Inflexibility*, S. Doc. 13, 74th Cong. 1st Sess., 1935; "Notes on Inflexible Prices," 26 (1) Am. Econ. Rev. Supp. 23 (March 1936).

On the contrary, the most competent economic opinion, as well in Europe as in this country, can be cited in support of the view that a strong contributing cause of the unparalleled severity of the present depression was the greatly increased extent of monopolistic control of commodity prices which stimulated financial speculation in the financial markets. There is growing doubt whether the capitalistic system, whose basic assumption is free markets and a free price system, can continue to work with an ever widening range of prices fixed or manipulated by monopolies.[77]

The committee of economists which prepared this defense of antitrust in 1932 was chaired, not surprisingly, by Frank Albert Fetter.[78] However, its six other sponsors represented a broad spectrum of policy views; they were were P. M. Atkins, E. L. Bogart, James Bonbright, I. L. Sharfman, Willard Thorp, and Jacob Viner. The resolution subsequently gained a total of 127 signatures including those of C. O. Hardy, Paul Douglas, J. B. Clark, Henry Schultz, Chester Wright, John R. Commons, Alvin Hanson, and Raymond Whittlesey. With more elaborate organization, the number of signatories would have been greater. The sponsoring committee generally contacted only one member of each academic department. The statement of Fetter's committee in 1932 can be taken as marking the most emotional phase of the love affair of American economists with antitrust. Fetter recorded that, among economists, he had only one completely negative reaction to the committee's statement; and that a number of distinguished figures declined to sign because of what, to him, were minor reservations about wording. Conspicuous by their absence were Frank Knight, Henry Simons, J. M. Clark, W. C. Mitchell, W. Z. Ripley, and Irving Fisher.

The Return of Doubt

OVER THE years, and especially after World War II at the University of Chicago, antitrust issues began to be studied by economists with much better training, tools, and, above all, better data. Even in the interwar years, a few seeds of doubt had begun to germinate. To Henry Simons, business monopoly was at worst a skin disorder, the dangerous malig-

[77]"Statement of the Economists' Committee on Anti-Trust Law Policy," 22 *Am. Econ. Rev.* 465, 468 (1932).
[78]Correspondence between Viner and Fetter confirms that Fetter took the initiative in forming the committee and drafted its statement. Jacob Viner Papers, Box 32, Princeton University Library.
[79]H. C. Simons, *Economic Policy for a Free Society* 130 (1948). Looking back, we know that Simons greatly overestimated the monopoly power of labor unions. I suspect that his Doomsday

nancy being labor monopoly.[79] J. M. Clark, as a result of his work as a consultant to the cement industry in connection with its legal problems, came to have doubts about the wisdom of using antitrust to attack basing-point systems of pricing.[80] The statistical analysis underpinning Gardiner Means' thesis that administered prices in high concentration industries were somehow different (and presumably more "monopolistic") than prices in low concentration industries had drawn criticism almost from its first appearance.[81]

After World War II, support for antitrust among economists began to erode, notwithstanding that its popularity with Congress and the courts was rising to a new peak. This is not really surprising. As J. M. Keynes reminded us, the ideas which civil servants and politicians "and even agitators" apply to current events are not likely to be the newest.[82] As noted earlier, empirical studies indicated, at most, a small effect of industry concentration on rates of return on capital. Studies of the deadweight welfare loss of monopoly that were based on austere but not unreasonable assumptions found it to be somewhere between small and trivial.[83] The widely accepted belief that industrial concentration had been increasing in the American economy for fifty years or more was found to be wrong.[84]

---

view was influenced by the factory occupations by workers and violence that accompanied many of the organizational strikes of the 1930s.

[80] J. M. Clark, "Imperfect Competition and Basing-Point Problems," 33 *Am. Econ. Rev.* 283 (1943).

[81] See, for example, D. D. Humphrey, "The Nature and Meaning of Rigid Prices, 1890–1933." 45 *J. Pol. Econ.* 651 (1937), and R. S. Tucker, "The Reasons for Price Rigidity," 28 *Am. Econ. Rev.* 41 (1938).

The definitive criticism of the Means thesis did not come until after World War II. See Richard Ruggles, "The Nature of Price Flexibility and the determinants of Relative Price Changes in the Economy," in Business Concentration and Price Policy, (National Bureau of Economic Research, 1955), p. 441.

Ruggles found that concentration had no apparent effect on price changes during the depression but rather that industries with the greatest percentage fall in prices were those whose costs were heavily weighted with outlays on farm products. In the depression, the output of major farm products actually increased as demand fell because farm employment increased. In the early depression, the normal export of labor from rural to urban areas was drastically reduced and most farm workers, being family members, could not be laid off.

[82] J. M. Keynes, *The General Theory of Employment, Interest, and Money* (1936), p. 384.

[83] Notably Arnold Harberger, "Monopoly and Resource Allocation," 44 *Am. Econ. Rev.* 77 (May 1954), and D. A. Worcester, "New Estimates of the Welfare Loss to Monopoly, 1956–1969," 40 *So. Econ. J.* 234 (1973).

For a bibliography of studies of welfare loss, see W. L. Baldwin, *Market Power, Competition, and Antitrust Policy,* (1987), p. 515.

[84] G. J. Stigler, "Competition in the United States," *Five Lectures on Economic Problems* (1950), p. 462; W. G. Nutter, *The Extent of Enterprise Monopoly in the United States, 1889–1939* (1951). In both studies, concentration ratios are used as proxies for monopoly.

An especially destructive blow to the economic case for antitrust was delivered by work which called into question the possibility of using predatory pricing to create a monopoly rent. No such rent can be gained by the would-be monopolist unless, having driven out rivals, he can take over their market share and hold it unchallenged for a time. But if the would-be monopolist and his rivals are assumed to have complete information about one another's cost and revenue functions, and an economic rent can be gained by the elimination of competition among themselves, they will merge or cartelize. In this way, they avoid the costs of a business "war." Given the complete absence of uncertainty, he who seeks a monopoly rent will only resort to predatory pricing as a second-best option, that is, when he is prevented by Law or Nature from employing a merger or cartel.[85]

If rival firms operate on the basis of incomplete information, as in the real world they do, business wars are always possible since there is no guaranty that they can agree on the terms of cooperation. An optimist may demand a bigger price for selling out than a pessimist is willing to pay. When negotiation fails, one party may seek to drive out the other and acquire his market share by quoting prices that, for a time, bear no relation to costs. Clearly. But there is no way of telling in advance whether economic welfare will be greater under legal rules that allow hard competition as against those that mandate soft competition. Hard competition may permit the creation of an entry barrier by increasing the perceived costs of entry. Soft competition may permit the emergence of excess capacity by making entry and survival easier for new firms. (Hard competition here means that permitted by the common law doctrine of "disinterested malevolence"—the doctrine ruling in British courts and American state courts before 1890).

The welfare merits of hard versus soft competition is a very difficult (and therefore very expensive) problem for empirical research. We now have, for the American economy, a vast amount of relevant evidence but most is of low quality—forty-year-old doctoral dissertations and FTC reports, studies done for Congressional committees with a bias in favor of small business etc. A price theorist who samples this literature will have no trouble in concluding that best evidence indicates that changes in law designed to soften competition, if they have any impact at all, injure consumers. But even best evidence incorporates mainly fragmentary and long

---

[85]That predatory price cutting is irrational on assumptions of perfect information and freedom of contract seems to have been first pointed out in print in W. A. Leeman, "The Limitations of Local Price-Cutting as a Barrier to Entry," 64 *J. Pol. Econ.* 329 (1956).

out-of-date statistics. For the present, it is unlikely that anyone's a priori views on the merits of hard versus soft competition will be changed by a study of the "facts."

In recent years, not all of the criticism of antitrust has come from economists who view it exclusively through the price theory perspective. The views of Oliver Williamson deriving from his emphasis on the firm's never ending effort to minimizing transaction costs are not quite so negative. Still, he does make clear that earlier generations of economists were too quick to label as anticompetitive innovations in business structure and conduct that could have no place in a perfectly competitive market.[86] When Williamson's perspective is employed, most of the business practices attacked under the antitrust laws as anticompetitive can be shown to have alternative explanations.[87]

The criticism of the economic case for antitrust, which was the work of many investigators, was summarized and forcefully set forth in the 1970s in influential books by Dom Armentano,[88] Richard Posner,[89] and Robert Bork.[90] Although differing on a few points, their main conclusion was the same; virtually no part of antitrust can be justified on economic grounds except the rule that price-fixing agreements are illegal per se. And even in the 1970s, Armentano was beginning to have doubts about the benefits of the per se rule.

---

[86]Oliver Williamson, *Markets and Hierarchies, Analysis and Antitrust Implications: A Study in the Economics of Internal Organization* (1975) and "The Modern Corporation: Origins, Evolution, Attributes," 19 *J. Econ. Literature* 1537 (1981).

[87]The older economists' case for antitrust still has its supporters, most notably in Walter Adams, J. W. Brock, and W. G. Shepherd. For that matter, it still influences the thinking of most economists, especially those who are only occasionally concerned with antitrust issues. See W. G. Shepherd, *The Treatment of Market Power: Antitrust, Regulation, and Public Enterprise* (1975), and Walter Adams and J. W. Brock, *The Bigness Complex: Industry, Labor, and Government in the American Economy* (1986).

Discussion between adherents of the economic case for antitrust and its critics is made difficult by the emotional baggage both groups bring to it. Most economists who hold to the old view dislike and distrust the leadership of the Fortune 500 companies, and this attitude has little to do with market share. Some skeptics believe that no amount of monopoly in the private sector of the economy is enough to warrant the expansion of State power needed to eliminate it. Nevertheless, a good faith effort should be made to put aside this emotional baggage. Viewed as a scientific problem, the strictly "economic" issues to be settled reduce to two empirical questions. (1) How much monopoly rent is there in the private sector? (2) Would it be cost effective to eliminate it?

[88]D. T. Armentano, *Antitrust Policy: The Case for Repeal* (1986).

[89]Richard Posner, *Antitrust Law: An Economic Perspective* (1976).

[90]Robert Bork, *The Antitrust Paradox: A Policy at War with Itself* (1978).

Antitrust and Technology

THERE IS one important area in which the work of economists, in recent years at least, has done the case for antitrust no harm. The view has been put forward, most eloquently and brashly by J. K. Galbraith, that that large firms with large market shares are the engines of economic progress.[91] Size gives them the resources to undertake grand projects and large market shares give them the incentives to do so.[92] Assuming that one prefers more economic progress to less, the implication of this view is that antitrust is good to the extent that it contributes to this goal and bad to the extent that it does not. So far, however, economists have not been able to establish a connection between antitrust and technological progress close enough to deserve to have an influence on policy.[93]

Here, economic theory speaks with forked tongue. The usual other things being equal, monopoly provides a greater incentive to a firm to invest in research and development because it permits the appropriation of whatever payoff is realized. Monopoly eliminates free riding on research. But competition encourages a more rapid adoption of new inventions once they have appeared from somewhere, because it more rapidly destroys the value of machines and products made obsolete by change. (In the days of its near national monopoly of telephone service before 1974, AT&T was well known both for its heavy investment in research and its slowness in bringing innovations on line.) In short, a typical tradeoff problem.

Presumably, for every industry, at every time and place, there exists an industry structure that is optimal for promoting technological progress. As yet, we do not know how to identify such a structure and it is unlikely that we ever will. Even if we could divine it, in a world of constant change, any structure that is optimal now will momentarily become suboptimal. Empirical studies seeking a connection between market structure and changing technology have turned up much quaint, curious, and intriguing information but no solid evidence that monopoly, when it can be found in the real world, is either a brake on, or a booster for, technological progress.

One possible inference from these inconclusive results is that so many factors affect the rate of technological progress—and the statistical problems are so difficult—that the tie between industry structure and tech-

---

[91]J. K. Galbraith, *American Capitalism* (1952).

[92]This benign view of the big oligopolist circulated in central Europe many years before it gained much attention on this side of the Atlantic. A notably purple encomium by Walter Rathenau was translated from the German as *In Days to Come* (1921).

[93]An excellent introduction to this tangled subject is M. I. Kamien and N. L. Schwartz, *Market Structure and Innovation* (1982).

nological change cannot be isolated with existing econometric techniques. Another possible inference is that all the studies were fatally flawed from the outset, in that they have used a concentration ratio (usually involving capital assets or value added) as the measure of monopoly when the meaningful variable was entry barrier or some proxy for it (e.g., supranormal rate of return on capital.) There is one other possibility, namely that the studies which have found scant monopoly power in the private sector of the economy reached a correct conclusion. If so, there is no real problem. Absent a significant degree of monopoly, it is illogical to expect that empirical work will tell us much about the tie between technological change and market structure.

Blue-ribbon opinion among economists on antitrust has come almost full circle. One can imagine the shade of William Graham Sumner, somewhere out there muttering "I warned you and you fools wouldn't listen."[94] (In life, Sumner was not known for his tact and forebearance.) Since the best work by economists on antitrust has only served to underscore the merits of laissez-faire—and, as we have seen, given the assumptions of price theory, it could not have been otherwise—two questions would seem to require answers. Was this trip necessary? What was learned along the way? I am most comfortable with the second question.

Microeconomics as an Externality of Antitrust

A STRONG case can be made that a great part of modern microeconomics is the creation of economists working in the United States; and that it has developed in response to our efforts to deal with issues forced on our attention by antitrust.[95] (Without antitrust, microeconomics no doubt could have developed in some other, quite possibly better, way, for example as an extension of international trade theory; the emotional environment of antitrust has tended to erode good scientific habits.) Among

---

[94] A representative sample of Sumner's ideology and irascibility can be found in two articles on trusts published in the *The Journal of Commerce and Commercial Bulletin* on June 24 and 25, 1901. Thus "there is no evil or danger in trusts which is nearly so menacing to society as the measures which are proposed for destroying trusts."

[95] My estimate that much, if not most, of modern microeconomics is an externality of the antitrust experiment would seem to contradict George Stigler's conclusion that it has had only minor influence on fundamental economic research. "The Economists and the Problem of Monopoly," 72 *Am. Econ. Rev.* 1 (May 1982).

Since Stigler's judgment is not elaborated and what is fundamental is a matter of taste, the reasons for this difference will not be pursued here. I will not refrain from pointing out that much of Stigler's life work, for which is he rightly honored, has been concerned with problems of monopoly whether real or, as his studies often showed, imaginary.

the issues that had to be thought through were those raised by cartels, oligopoly, price discrimination, mergers, resale price maintenance, vertical integration, tying contracts, so-called predatory competition, free riding, and limit pricing. As a recent example of a benign externality of the Sherman Act, I would cite the theory of contestable markets which grew out the consulting activities of William Baumol and his associates.[96] The conclusion seems justified that while antitrust has done nothing provable to benefit consumers, it has certainly helped to educate economists.

In considering the other question—was this trip necessary—we should remember that many, if not most, of the economic issues raised by antitrust appeared in court before they had received the attention of economists. The Supreme Court had the task of trying to figure out the meaning of price leadership in *United States Steel* in 1920.[97] The justices would have been no wiser if they had consulted the leading economics textbooks of that day. A nineteenth-century court wrestled with the welfare implications of a tying contract before economists had even heard of the problem.[98] Economists had nothing to say about resale price maintenance until after the practice was condemned by the Supreme Court in *Dr. Miles*.[99]

We should remember that the Sherman Act is older than what is usually regarded as "big business." It is even older by a few months than Alfred Marshall's *Principles of Economics,* which is the classic treatment of markets populated by family firms producing specialty products. In 1890, most American economists knew their Adam Smith, David Ricardo, John Stuart Mill, and maybe Francis Amasa Walker. But their knowledge of economic theory did not extend very far beyond these writers, and one suspects that some of the Germanophiles among them did not even know this much. When it came to information about the economic system, American econ-

---

[96] W. J. Baumol, "Contestable Markets: An Uprising in the Theory of Industrial Structure," 72 *Am. Econ. Rev.* 72 (1982), and W. J. Baumol, J. C. Panzar, and R. D. Willig, *Contestable Markets and the Theory of Industry Structure,* rev. ed. (1988).

At the limit, a contestable market is one in which, for producers, there are no barriers to entry and exit is costless; that is, a market which is never more than seconds away from an efficient, zero profit, equilibrium. There has been much criticism of contestable market theory as "unrealistic," but such criticism is bad science. All intellectual constructions are unrealistic since they involve abstraction. In common with every other bit of price theory, contestable market theory is useful for understanding some parts of reality and ill-suited to other parts. Clearly the (officially) illegal taxi industry of New York City where drivers can rent their cabs by the day, is highly contestable. Coal mining is not. In any event, Baumol and company, by pointing out the significance of exit costs for decisions of the firm, cleared up a major ambiguity in price theory.

[97] *United States v. United States Steel Corp.,* 251 U.S. 417 (1920).

[98] *Heaton-Peninsular Button-Fastener v. Eureka Specialty Co.,* 77 Fed. 288 (1896).

[99] *Dr. Miles Medical Co. v. Park & Sons Co.,* 220 U.S. 373 (1911).

omists in 1890 knew little more than did American Congressmen and journalists. The American Economic Association only emerged from the membership of the American Historical Association in the summer of 1885.

Is it a reproach to our profession that we have traveled from William Graham Sumner by way of Frank Albert Fetter only to wind up with the modern skepticism? I think not. Our education—and the resulting expertise—was obtained at a reasonable cost to the public. For its first fifty years, the country's investment in antitrust was so small that its welfare impact, whether positive or negative, had to have been slight. Antitrust became a policy with an unmistakable price tag only after World War II, with the rise of the treble damage suit, the class action, and the growing power of the antitrust agencies to block mergers.

Economists are entitled to plead that, if our learning was slow, the problems were tough and the pressures for quick answers many; and that we did the best we could with little data and primitive theoretical and statistical techniques. After all, until 1928, no economist had published a marginal revenue curve,[100] and until 1934, none had estimated profit rates for American manufacturing industries.[101] The first statistical estimates of concentration trends at the industry level in the United States did not appear until the early 1950s.[102] No estimate of the actual profitability of illegal collusion in the economy was published until 1976.[103]

Perhaps the rate of learning about antitrust would have been greater if Sumner had had a less acerbic personality, if John Maurice Clark had paid more attention to his father's early doubts, and if the case for antitrust had not been taken up by economists who were both professionally eminent and able publicists. In addition to Fetter and the Clarks, this group included William Z. Ripley,[104] Allyn Young,[105] Henry Simons,[106] Corwin Edwards,[107] Fritz Machlup,[108] and, in his youth at least, George Stigler.[109]

---

[100] T. O. Yntema, "The Influence of Dumping on Monopoly Price," 36 *J. Pol. Econ.* 686 (1928).

[101] R. C. Eptstein, *Industrial Profits in the United States* (1934). Epstein estimated the rate of return on total capital for 73 manufacturing industries for 1924–28.

[102] G. J. Stigler, "Competition in the United States," *Five Lectures on Economic Problems*, (1950), p. 46; W. G. Nutter, *The Extent of Enterpise Monopoly in the United States, 1889–1939* (1951).

[103] Peter Asch and J. J. Seneca. "Is Collusion Profitable?" 58 *Rev. Econ. Stat.* 1 (1976).

[104] W. Z. Ripley, *Main Street and Wall Street* (1927).

[105] A. A. Young, "The Sherman Act and the New Anti-Trust Legislation," 23 *J. Pol. Econ.* 201, 305, 417 (1915).

[106] H. C. Simons, *Economic Policy for a Free Society* (1948).

[107] C. D. Edwards, *Maintaining Competition* (1949).

[108] Fritz Machlup, *The Political Economy of Monopoly* (1952).

[109] See, for example, G. J. Stigler, "The Statistics of Merger and Monopoly," 64 *J. Pol. Econ.* 33 (1956).

Mea Culpa?

HAVE THE mistakes of economists been costly in the sense that they have led to the adoption of unwise (i.e., welfare-destroying) antitrust rules? Assuming that judges and legislators were paying attention to us some of the time, our bad advice must have done some harm. For example, it provided fallacious arguments for the merger and price discrimination provisions of the Clayton Act. It encouraged the antitrust agencies to bring cases against firms that used basing points and zones in preparing price lists, even though there was no evidence that the alternatives would do more for economic welfare. It popularized the notion that oligopoly—any market occupied by only a few sellers—is evidence of "shared monopoly."

Yet here again, I see no reason to grovel in guilt. In giving advice that later turned out to be bad, economists are hardly alone among the professions. In any event, judges, legislators, and civil servants would have reached most of our incorrect conclusions about antitrust without our help. The most influential errors were (and are) enticingly plausible, e.g., the belief that consumers are bound to lose when manufacturers refuse to deal with retailers who do not respect suggested price markups.

In the past, I have argued that "antitrust comes a cost." While I certainly still think so, the statement needs to be carefully qualified. It is true in one sense only; that the introduction of antitrust rules which restrict mergers, cartels, and exclusionary pricing into a laissez-faire model must reduce economic welfare as economists understand the term. Of this, there is no doubt. But to say the obvious, we cannot know what would have happened to the American economy without the antitrust experiment. In its absence, the political dissatisfaction with the results of laissez-faire could—and, in my opinion, probably would—have produced policies even more destructive of economic welfare. Regulation by public utility commission and State-owned monopoly are always waiting in the wings. And these two alternatives are policies that over time build up rent-collecting vested interests in a way that antitrust does not.

We should note one argument in favor of antitrust that has a certain plausibility even though it is, at present, immune to quantification. According to the argument, antitrust is the one governmental policy that stands in stark contrast to the multitude of federal, state, and local policies that accommodate the rent-seeking activities of politically influential groups. The existence of antitrust is held to serve as a permanent reminder that these policies are presumptively suspect and can be justified, if at all, only by "special circumstances." Maybe so. But skeptics are entitled to respond with an equally plausible and nontestable argument: the antitrust effort has been a monumental distraction that has encouraged the search for monopoly rents and resource misallocation in the wrong places. In a world franchise values created by government, why worry about the marketing of household liquid bleach (water plus an additive)[110] or the merger plans of a local grocery chain in the automobile age?[111] Or so the argument goes.

The Reagan Years

IN ITS first hundred years the antitrust experiment of the United States achieved its greatest popularity in Congress and the courts between 1965 and 1975, that is, in a decade when its support among economists was rapidly eroding and twenty years or more after its peak popularity in the profession. On taking office, the Reagan administration made a serious and quite successful effort to move antitrust in the direction of contemporary blue-ribbon opinion in economics. To this end, conglomerate and vertical mergers were left alone as were horizontal mergers involving small market shares. Prosecution of price-fixing agreements was vigorously pushed. And the Justice Department sought (unsuccessfully) to overturn the rule in *Dr. Miles* against resale price maintenance contracts.[112]

Will the Reagan course be maintained in future administrations? My guess is that it will not. I also suspect that a change in direction will not carry policy back to the highwater mark of antitrust in the 1960s as registered in *Clorox*,[113] *Brown Shoe*,[114] *Utah Pie*,[115] and the like. Some movement toward the past is to be expected given that the suspicion of "big business" has not gone away. Nor has the populist impulse in American politics—the wish to discomfort the rich and powerful without seriously threatening their persons or property. It has been with us since the Plymouth Colony. Even with treble damage suits and class actions on the scale of the early 1980s, antitrust is still a low-cost way of providing an outlet for the impulse. Whatever the welfare losses of antitrust, they are certainly less than those imposed on the economy by the tax policies and zoning regulations of three levels of government.

Still, it is not likely that the Reagan impact on antitrust will be completely erased in the near future. The opinion of economists does matter if only because we are the teachers of judges, Congressmen, civil ser-

---

[110]*Federal Trade Commission v. Procter & Gamble Co.*, 386 U.S. 568 (1967).
[111]*United States v. Von's Grocery Co.*, 384 U.S. 270 (1966).
[112]*Monsanto Co. v. Spray-Rite Corp.*, 465 U.S. 752 (1984).
[113]*Federal Trade Commission v. Proctor & Gamble Co.*, 386 U.S. 568 (1967).
[114]*Brown Shoe Co. v. United States*, 370 U.S. 294 (1962).
[115]*Utah Pie Co. v. Continental Baking Co. et al.*, 386 U.S. 685 (1967).

vants—and law professors. Except for the belief that good work is done by suppressing cartels, the faith of earlier generations of economists in antitrust is largely gone. Add, too, that belief in antitrust as a way of helping consumers presupposes a closed economy; it must decline as the importance of imports and exports increases. A proposal to break up General Motors as a way of lowering automobile prices could be (and was) seriously debated at professional meetings in the 1950s when import competition was nonexistent for the firm. In the 1990s, such a proposal is, on its face, simply silly.

The Way Ahead

AN ECONOMIST is honor bound to give as honest a reading as he can of the costs and benefits of antitrust in relation to proposed alternatives. As we have seen, when the organon employed is price theory, and the alternative for comparison is freer exchange, the economist will, if his syllogisms are sound, always rule against antitrust—in the absence of evidence that justifies setting aside one or more of the basic assumptions of price theory. But the eoncomist as citizen has no obligation to preach Bork's output test (chapter 7) or Dewey's welfare test (chapter 8). Decentralization of decision-making, the dispersion of power, and a higher standard of business ethics are honorable values. Antitrust has done something to advance them in the past and can do so in the future. There is no reason why the Law's reasonable man should not conclude that antitrust, with all its presumptive inefficiencies, is not worth the cost.

Recently Dominick Armentano has taken the dedicated price theorist's last logical step and called for the repeal of the antitrust laws.[116] Total repeal is, of course, out of the question because the corporation is a creation of law whose rights and responsibilities have to be specified somewhere. Libertarians of Armentano's convictions, with their profound distrust of the State, have trouble coming to terms with the truth that only the State can create a corporate "person" and endow it with rights. As an accident of history, the Sherman Act became the statutory basis for much of the early federal efforts at the supervision and control of corporations. Clearly the American experiment with antitrust would never have taken its present form if the federal government in 1890 had had a monopoly on the chartering of corporations doing an interstate business.[117]

---

[116]D. T. Armentano, *Antitrust Policy: The Case for Repeal* (1986).

[117]Allyn Young, a staunch supporter of antitrust, doubted the wisdom of the Clayton and Federal Trade Commission Acts because he feared their passage would postpone the day when the federal government would take the sensible step of taking over the chartering of

Repeal of Sherman and its children would have to coincide with new statutory foundations for many of the federal oversight functions that they now support. Thus even if price-fixing agreements were decriminalized, it would still be necessary to decide which, if any, of them would be enforceable in court. Antitrust and patent law are now so thoroughly entwined that patent law would have to be rewritten if antitrust were to go. Still, as an administrative matter, much of antitrust could be dismantled—and the Reagan years have pointed the way. The important obstacle to change is the widespread (and well-founded) fear that dismantling would be followed by developments, most notably the rapid cartelization of the economy, that would scare the wits out of most Americans—including most Congressmen and, probably, most economists as well.

And the future? The per se rule against price-fixing agreements seems safe enough into the next century. No whisper has been heard against it in the courts or Congress since *Appalachian Coals* (1933)[118] and the demise of the NRA in 1935. Nevertheless, even in this area of antitrust the climate of ideas seems to be changing. An American law journal for the first time ever (so far as I know) recently carried an article calling not only for repeal of the per se rule but also for an amendment that would direct the courts to enforce price-fixing agreements that are likely to increase economic welfare.[119] The author, John Lopatka, did not go into details about how good cartels were to be distinguished from bad ones.

The per se rule against price fixing is no exception to the presumption derived from price theory that all restrictions on freedom of contract reduce economic welfare. As yet, most economists support the rule either because they have had no occasion to think about it (the more common case), or because they are persuaded by the empirical evidence offered on its behalf. Such evidence, based mainly on casual empiricism, is increasingly being called into question.[120] Still, whatever its actual impact on welfare, cooperation among rival firms to set prices, divide markets, or plan

---

large corporations. "The Sherman Act and the New Anti-Trust Legislation," 23 *J. Pol. Econ.* 417 (1915). Young also had other reservations about the 1914 laws, especially Clayton, which he rightly saw as terribly muddy.

[118] *Appalachian Coals, Inc. v. United States,* 288 U.S. 344 (1933). Here a Supreme Court, badly shaken by the depression, allowed 137 bituminous coal producers in the eastern region to set up a cooperative marketing program in the hope of staving off even more bankruptcies. The Court reasonably concluded that the participants were more to be pitied than censured.

[119] J. E. Lopatka, "The Case for Legal Enforcement of Price Fixing Agreements," 38 *Emory L.J.* 1 (1989).

[120] See, for example, George Bittlingmayer, "Decreasing Average Cost and Competition: A New Look at the Addyston Pipe Case," 25 *J. Law Econ.* 201 (1982) and C. M. Newmark, "Is Antitrust Enforcement Effective?," 96 *J. Pol. Econ.* 1111 (1988).

investment smacks too much of an unfair ganging up on unorganized consumers—unless, of course, the consumers happen to be foreigners. Courts
and legislatures have always looked more favorably on cartel agreements
covering products to be sold outside their jurisdictions.

The ad hoc scrutiny of mergers by the antitrust agencies will continue
under the guise of applying somebody's merger guidelines. (All that price
theory does for merger evaluation is provide a presumption that the loosest
guidelines are best.) The de facto burden of proof, when a merger is chal-
lenged, can be expected to shift back and forth between government and
defendant as popular attitudes toward big business warm and cool. The
antitrust agencies received a broad grant of power in the Hart-Scott-Ro-
dino Act (1976) to delay mergers.[121] As one would expect, it has been used
to persuade firms to revise their proposals in ways thought desirable in
order to expedite approval and reduce the risk of challenge to the merger
in court. This "fixing" of mergers before clearance by civil servants now
seems to be an accepted part of antitrust enforcement and likely to continue.

More uncertain—and more important to the actual functioning of the
economy—is the future of the treble damage suit, since each year far more
firms are threatened, or hit, with private suits than tangle with the federal
government. The development of private remedies is largely in the hands
of trial courts and juries—institutions whose behavior is notoriously difficult to predict.

One judicial drift in civil litigation deserves mention here. In recent years,
the courts have indicated a willingness to narrow the doctrine that provides
immunity from antitrust to the actions of state and local governments that
would be violations of the Sherman Act if done by private parties.[122] Given
the important role of state and local governments in rent creation, this is—
or was—a development of truly revolutionary possibilities. (Hundreds of
bankrupt municipalities? Liens on public parks? Taxes imposed by federal
courts to pay damage awards?) However, the possibilities so alarmed Congress that, in 1984, the right to sue the states and their subdivisions for
damages under antitrust was virtually eliminated. To save themselves and
their localities from liability, officials need only show that they acted in
good faith. The much less valuable right to sue for injunctive relief remains.[123]

---

[121]90 Stat. 1383 (1976).

[122]*In Parker v. Brown,* 317 U.S. 341 (1943), the Supreme Court appeared to confer a total
immunity from antitrust suits on anything done under the cover of state law. However, in
a number of later cases, this blanket protection was reduced, especially for units of local
government. See, for example, *City of Lafayette v. Louisiana Power and Light Co.,* 435 U.S.
389 (1978); *Community Communications Co., Inc. v. City of Boulder,* 455 U.S. 40 (1982); and
324 Liquor Corp. v. Duffy, 479 U.S. 335 (1987).

[123]Local Government Antitrust Act, 98 Stat. 2750 (1984).

The incidence of "big" divestiture suits has declined over the last thirty years and, with the manpower of the antitrust agencies increasingly devoted to screening mergers and harassing cartels, I would not expect a revival in their popularity. Still, since 1890 every decade has usually produced at least one such suit. The occasional sacrificial lamb from the corporate world will probably continue to be offered up to propitiate influential legislators, to keep faith with ideology, or simply because a big divestiture case provides civil servants with a welcome change from the monotony of screening mergers and prosecuting price-fixing conspirators.

Economists have learned an immense amount about real world markets by studying antitrust issues over the last century. I think that the learning experience is now pretty far into dimishing returns. In the future, I expect that our role in analyzing antitrust will be very similar to our role in analyzing problems of tariff protection. We will point out the costs and, on occasion, try to measure them. Some of us will demonstrate ingenuity by devising scenarios in which, by the careful choice of assumptions, an antitrust rule brought forward by lawyers can be shown to increase economic welfare—just as clever international trade theorists, can construct models to show that a nation can sometimes increase its economic welfare by the correct mixture of tariffs, exchange controls, and bargaining strategies.

The truth is that much of what passes for economic analysis in antitrust cases, has come to be a kind of window dressing. Thus in *Du Pont-General Motors*[124] the "real" issue was whether, because of their size, the corporate tie between the country's largest automobile manufacturer and its largest chemical company should be allowed to continue. A bow in the direction of economics required the Court to sift through a mountain of irrelevant statistics on the market for automobile paints and varnishes before concluding that the tie should be cut. The government contention was that the tie gave Du Pont an unfair advantage over other paint producers in selling to General Motors. So far as I know, no economist or statistician has ever suggested that the outcome of the case made any perceptible difference to the prices of cars and trucks.

From the beginning, two seldom-voiced presumptions about antitrust enforcement have contended for favor in the courts and Congress. One says that all doubts should be resolved in favor of freedom of contract—provided that the cost is not too great. The other says that all doubts should be resolved in favor of decentralized decision-making—provided that the cost is not too great. Arguments of great weight and antiquity can be cited to support both. Given the obstacles to measuring cost—and the oppor-

---

[124] *United States v. E. I. DuPont de Nemours & Co.,* 353 U.S. 586 (1957).

tunities that antitrust provides for good and inexpensive political theater—
I can see no reason why the contest between these two quite reasonable
presumptions should ever be finally decided.

Provided that the constraint "so long as the cost is not too great" is
accepted, as it mostly has been by the courts and Congress, the American
political consensus can accommodate any version of antitrust that has ever
been seriously proposed—even the extremes advocated by Robert Bork
and Justice Douglas. The one event that might be cited to call into question
the enduring conservative tilt in antitrust enforcement is the breakup of
the national telephone system by consent decree in 1982. However, for the
reasons indicated below, the AT&T case had so many unusual and acci-
dental features that it should, I believe, be treated as an aberration and not
as evidence that the unwritten rules of the antitrust game have changed.[125]

The Strange Fate of Ma Bell

IN THE history of antitrust, the AT&T case is absolutely unique in two
respects. First, AT&T at the start of the suit in November, 1974, was
collecting far more monopoly rent than any firm that the government had

---

[125]Dispassionate, though sympathetic, accounts of Ma Bell's series of misfortunes leading up
to the 1982 consent decree are Steve Coll, *The Deal of the Century: The Breakup of AT&T*
(1986), and Peter Temin, *The Fall of the Bell System* (1987). A bitter but illuminating lament
by two veteran Bell engineers is C. R. Krause and A. W. Duerig, *The Rape of Ma Bell: The
Criminal Wrecking of the Best Telephone System in the World* (1988).

The ironies of the case were many. Consider the following. The case was begun on the
initiative of civil servants who had two main goals. They wished to reduce the Bell system's
power to protect its share of the market for long-distance voice and data transmission (close
to 100 percent in the 1960s) against the inroads of Microwave Communications, Incorporated
(MCI). And they wished to compel the system to spin off its manufacturing subsidary, Western Electric. After MCI, a competitor whose costs per unit of service were initially above
AT&T's because of low traffic density, had gained a market foothold, the case was concluded
under a chief of the Antitrust Division, William Baxter, who wished to free AT&T from
the regulatory control of the Federal Communications Commission. According to Baxter's
scenario, AT&T could then use whatever cost advantages remained after its adaptation to an
unregulated market in competition with all comers. To this end, long-distance telephone
service was separated from local service which, by common consent, had to remain under
government regulation. Because of Congressional opposition, Baxter's hope has not been
realized and, in fact, was never politically feasible. Only some form of federal regulation can
protect the providers of long-distance service and their customers against the monopoly power
of the Baby Bells whose networks they must use.

The efforts of the Antitrust Division to separate long lines and Western Electric from AT&T
failed because AT&T's management was adamant about keeping them together in order to
participate in the "communications revolution" (despite the handicap of a legacy of career
experience gained in a sheltered, regulated industry). Baxter did not think the separation was
important enough to hold up a settlement.

ever attacked in the past. When the case began, AT&T was by far the largest privately owned firm in the world with over a million employees. It was well insulated by government regulation against the challenges of would-be competitors. It had a virtual monopoly of long distance telephone service and, in most areas of the country, a complete monopoly of local telephone service as well. Second, the costs of divestiture imposed on the firm's employees and customers (but not on its stockholders) were greater than in any previous exercise in trust-busting. While in 1911 divestiture decree in *Standard Oil* created more new firms and radically altered the structure of the oil industry, the effects only gradually became apparent over a period of thirty years; in the first phase, each of the regional Standard companies retained its exclusive sales territory and whatever monopoly rent it was collecting.

Already in the 1960s the Federal Communications Commission, over Ma Bell's vehement opposition, had limited her power to dictate the types of equipment that customers could plug into the telephone network. Her troubles began in earnest when, in 1974, a tiny company, Microwave Communications, Incorporated (MCI), by brilliant entrepreneurship and legal maneuvering managed to break her monopoly of long-distance telephone service. This it did by using microwave technology to transmit messages between cities and plugging into the local telephone network at both ends. MCI managed to establish itself as a provider of long-distance service to the general public before the FCC discovered the operation. A gullible, or careless, FCC had thought that it had only authorized private line service that plugged into AT&T's local network.

MCI's entry and survival was made possible by several circumstances despite the inherent competitive advantages of AT&T, e.g., its far greater backup capacity. Regulation policy had set AT&T's long-distance rates on many routes above both marginal and average cost, the regulators insisting that the same rate be charged to users on high-cost, low-density routes as on low-cost, high-density routes. AT&T's equipment and technology were not state-of-the art. (Since AT&T was a protected monopolist, there was no reason why they should have been.) And AT&T had allowed an "unmet need" to develop in data transmission; the old firm was correctly perceived as slowing the introduction of the innovations that were coming fast and furious in telecommunications. AT&T reacted to the challenge from MCI in predictable fashion. It sought to kill the entrant with cuts in long-distance rates but was blocked by an FCC which was becoming increasingly reluctant to be seen as favoring AT&T. Another player in the long-distance market soon appeared in the form of the Southern Pacific Corporation providing the Sprint service.

The gravamen of the government's case against AT&T was quite simple. It alleged a type of behavior that any economist would regard as perfectly rational for a public utility subject to rate and service regulation. AT&T was charged with using its monopoly of telephone service to (1) stop potential competitors from challenging its control of long distance data and voice transmissions and (2) insure that only equipment supplied by itself would be installed in the telephone network on the feeble pretext that such exclusivity was necessary to protect the network from damage.[126] (Some of AT&T's critics accept that the firm's insistence on a Bell-only procurement policy may have had an engineering justification in the distant past.) Both charges were supported by a wealth of convincing evidence. The necessity that somebody must have a monopoly of local telephone service was not called into question.

While Ma Bell was a rent-collecting monopolist, she was a very peculiar one. The regulatory constraints under which she operated limited the rent that could be collected and caused it to be parceled out among stockholders, favored customers, and employees and consumed by the "goldplating" of telephone service. (The term is William Vickrey's.) The goal of goldplating was the not ignoble one of insuring extremely reliable service and good public relations. It took the form of hiring, carefully training, and closely surpervising high grade labor in generous amounts, over-engineering to minimize the risk of service interuptions, and the maintenance of backup capacity by accelerated investment. In this way, Ma Bell was able to obtain a higher level of rates, earn a reputation as a model employer, and enjoy a more comfortable organizational life than would have been possible in a more competitive environment. Not surprisingly, government lawyers made no effort to show the connection between the goldplating of telephone service and monopoly rent; indeed, they felt it nec-

---

[126] AT&T's insistence on manufacturing all equipment used in its network was rational within the context of regulation because it afforded a wealth of opportunities to "pad the rate base." The operating companies, while subject to rate regulation, were constitutionally entitled to a "fair rate of return on a fair valuation of investment." Unless regulators were eternally vigilant, fully informed about costs, and adequately funded, investment valuation—the rate base—could be increased and higher rates obtained by transferring equipment from the manufacturing subsidiary, Western Electric, to the operating companies at inflated bookkeeping markups.

There were, of course, some economies of vertical integration. There always are in a vertically integrated firm. But the speed with which AT&T customers and the Baby Bells diversified away from Western Electric as an equipment supplier when able to do so, casts doubt on the importance of these economies. It is hard to believe that they were great enough to explain the ferocity with which AT&T fought to retain its monopoly of the supply of telephone equipment.

essary to argue that service could be improved by measures that would reduce monopoly.

As the largest private firm in the world and a regulated public utility, the management of Ma Bell had little to fear from rival firms, disgruntled stockholders, or corporate raiders. Her only natural enemies were consumer activists who pressed for more restrictive federal and state regulation and antitrust enthusiasts who wished to destroy her. The relationship of Ma Bell and her state and federal regulators, though occasionally adversarial (notably in California) was inescapably symbiotic. She wanted no encroachment on her monopoly. Regulators wished an arrangment that minimized consumer complaints. Ma Bell's reliable service and willingness to provide any rate structure that was politically popular (which was generally one favoring households that made mainly local calls) gave the regulators what they wanted most. The fraction of monopoly rent going to AT&T stockholders had long since been capitalized in securities prices. Regulation and AT&T's expenditure policies combined to insure that the capital gains of stockholders did not increase at a rate which would attract legislative hostility.

The consent decree accepted by Judge Harold Greene in January 1982 had two main organizational results. From local service, it split off three units to form a new firm with the AT&T name—long lines, Bell laboratories, and Western Electric. It rearranged the twenty-four local telephone companies into seven independent regional monopolies (the Baby Bells) and severely restricted their ancillary activities. To the irritation of millions of households, the Baby Bells were at first not allowed to sell or repair equipment.

The breakup of the Bell System inevitably produced thousands of winners and thousands of losers. Was there any increase in economic welfare as economists understand the term? For the present the answer, I think, has to be: possibly, but probably not.

The reason for this doubt is simply that the core of Ma Bell's monopoly power was not destroyed but only bequeathed and divided among the Baby Bells. In the divestiture, the Baby Bells received approximately three-fourths of the old lady's assets. Local telephone service everywhere remains a state protected monopoly. Long-distance service cannot operate without access to local networks at each end. Absent government regulation, there would be a bargaining game between local and long-distance companies over the division of revenues, with the advantage going to the locals. And the more long-distance companies in existence, the greater the local's advantage. Absent regulation, at the limit of perfect competition in long-distance service, all monopoly rent not dissipated in excess capacity would go to local companies in access charges.

By the consent decree of 1982, anyone owning a share of AT&T stock received prorated shares in the eight new firms created by divestiture. To date, stockholders who retained the full complement of new securities have suffered no losses incontrovertibly due to the breakup—further evidence, if any is needed, that most, if not all, of Ma Bell's monopoly power was handed on to her children.

Employees of the Baby Bells were relatively untouched by divestiture. For example, at Nynex, which serves New York state and lower New England, employment increased from 94,900 in December 1984 to 97,400 in December 1988.[127] Further south, at Bell Atlantic, employment rose in this four-year period from 79,500 to 81,000.[128] The fate of employees who found themselves in the new AT&T organization was another matter.

In the four years after 1984, normal attrition, layoffs, and early retirements reduced new AT&T's personnel by a brutal 17 percent—from 365,200 to 304,200.[129] No doubt, some part of the cost savings that resulted from the reduction in employment signified an elimination of monopoly rent, especially that fraction of the fall that can be traced to the Baby Bells' new freedom to buy equipment elsewhere. But some of the job loss at new AT&T resulted because restraints imposed by the consent decree, together with FCC rulings, forced it to yield market share to rivals in the long-distance market. This transfer, of course, imposed a welfare loss insofar as it was associated with the creation of excess capacity.

If the assessment is correct that little or no monopoly power was destroyed by the Bell breakup, its impact on economic welfare will be determined by how it affects the goals and efficiency of regulation. It is difficult to see how divestiture can have affected the goals of regulation. Regulators still wish a constituency of contented consumers. This is most readily achieved by a return to something like the goldplated service of Ma Bell. The consent decree did enshrine a new permanent conflict—a struggle over the division of long-distance revenues between the Baby Bells and the suppliers of long distance service. In the first instance, this has meant a transfer of power from the state regulators to the FCC which sets the access charge that the Baby Bells can obtain for the use of their networks. Conflict over the access charge may ultimately vest power in Congressional committees that oversee telecommunications. Whether the

---

[127] Nynex, *Annual Report*, 1988.
[128] Bell Atlantic, *Annual Report*, 1988.
[129] AT&T, *Annual Report*, 1988.

transfer of key regulatory decisions from the state to the federal level will ultimately increase or decrease economic welfare remains to be seen.

As for efficiency in administration, regulators have historically preferred to deal with big, highly centralized units because they are easier (cheaper) to police. Divestiture goes against this conventional wisdom and, in the AT&T case, was opposed by all state regulatory commissions and the FCC. However, there is no reason why decentralization cannot be an aid to regulation if there is a will to make use of it. The FCC is now in a position to use rivalry among firms providing long-distance service to collect more accurate information on cost and revenue functions than was possible in Ma Bell's day. And a comparison of the performances of the Baby Bells ought to tell the regulators something useful. The separation of the Baby Bells from Western Electric reduces the possiblity of using vertical integration to pad the rate base. This should make it easier for regulators to value correctly the industry's capital investment for rate-making purposes.

Our verdict on the AT&T case must be, I think, that it represents no break in the tradition of using antitrust to seek decentralization of decision-making and dispersion of power under the guise of attacking monopoly. Given the strength of the populist tradition in this country, Ma Bell's outlandish size and conspicuous involvement in politics made her a natural target for trust busters. It is a tribute to her unique set of engineering, organizational, and political skills that she was able to survive as long as she did in the shadow of the Sherman Act.

Any reduction of monopoly rent produced by the breakup of the company was most likely pure serendipity. Admittedly, the case is unique in that it blighted so many thousands of careers and inconvenienced so many millions of consumers. But hardly anybody involved in the case seems to have intended this result—certainly not the idealistic lawyers of the Justice Department who first began it. The harm was done because the killing of Ma Bell was such an uncoordinated enterprise—and so much affected by chance events and improbable personalities. The very size of Ma Bell insures that we shall not see a comparable adventure in trust-busting for many years to come.

Final Thoughts

WHAT HAVE we learned from the first hundred years of the antitrust experiment? By my reading, the most important lessons are the following.

First, genuine, unambiguous, issues of "monopoly power" in the application of the antitrust laws to the unregulated, private sector of the

American economy are hardly ever present. Except in a few markets where entry barriers can be maintained for years at a time by violence and threats of violence (private trash collection in some Long Island towns), any misallocation of resources resulting from the exercise of monopoly power in the private, unregulated, sector must be presumed to be slight. This is so because monopoly rents—the only sure and certain evidence that monopoly power is at work—are so difficult to detect. There is no basis for assuming that government intervention to eliminate monopoly power in this sector will be cost effective.

Second, while enclaves of monopoly rent in the American economy are easy enough to find, most owe their existence to the patronage of the State and been placed beyond the reach of antitrust by the federal courts' broad interpretation of the state action doctrine and Congressional reluctance to see it narrowed. For better or worse, any effort to make antitrust into a serious antimonopoly policy (as distinct from a policy for decentralizing decision-making and improving business behavior) must involve limitations on the rent-creating activities of state and local legislatures. And this, of course, means a further transfer of power from elected officials to federal judges and civil servants. How far and how fast one is prepared to move along this road in the hope of increasing economic welfare depends upon a great many things—not excluding one's idea of the good society.

Third, even if there were monopoly rents in the unregulated, private sector worth bothering about, they would, with the passing of time, be capitalized into asset prices and transferred by sale to owners who were not responsible for their creation. In a world of organized capital markets, the only people who gain from the creation of monopoly are those who get in on the ground floor; latecomers buy their monopoly rents at competitive prices. Indeed, it is the absence of capitalized monopoly rents that makes trust-busting—divestiture of going concerns—politically possible, since no great loss is inflicted upon anybody. The ideal candidate for dissolution is the firm that has constant unit cost over a wide range of output and is earning a "normal" rate of return on capital. Its dissolution into, say, two firms cannot be presumed to affect either industry efficiency or earnings. (In the real world, a regional or national grocery chain closely approximates such an ideal candidate.) Of course, dissolution of a going concern in such a case will have some effect on efficiency and earnings, if only because a new set of top managers emerges. For a time, trust-busting lowers the age of top management. As in the case of the Baby Bells created by the AT&T decree in 1982, this development is usually associated with more experimentation in the way that business is done—though not necessarily with higher earnings.

Fourth, there can be no final and conclusive judgment on the economic costs and benefits of antitrust. Here, measurement is very difficult and therefore very costly. But even if measurement were easy and cheap, our final judgment about antitrust would still have to depend on what we thought the real world alternatives were. We can easily imagine policies both better and worse for promoting economic welfare. Whether the antitrust experiment is viewed as success or failure as a promoter of welfare depends on the answer that one gives to the question: what would have happened had it never been tried? As already indicated, my reading is that, with all its costs, antitrust did much, especially in its early years, to insure that widespread dissatisfaction with laissez-faire did not produce the responses of State-owned monopoly and public utility regulation.

Finally, at the highest level of abstraction, the explanation of antitrust is simply the dissatisfaction of legislators, judges, and juries with certain results that laissez-faire has produced when operating through the fragmented business law peculiar to the American federal system. These unpopular results form a mixed bag. Of the most easily identified, the most important are cartels, mergers that seem to be a by-product of stock market speculation, high concentration ratios in some markets, corporate bureaucracies that have no obvious efficiency justifications, and hard, indeed by modern standards of decency, brutal, competition in many markets. Because antitrust has been used to apply so many different correctives to so many different effects of laissez-faire, generalization about its aims is difficult and an elegant "theory of antitrust" is an impossibility. A follower of Robert Bork will see this lack of coherence as deplorable but quite inevitable, once the courts refuse to ground antitrust on a strict adherence to price theory and its implicit welfare tests. An admirer of Justice Holmes will see it as one more bit of evidence for his view that the life of the law is not logic but experience.

This chapter should not end on a note that could be mistaken for cynicism. There is much of popular myth and illusion in antitrust. The same is true of many other policies and institutions (notably the Federal Reserve System). But, in the case of antitrust, the myth and illusion has therapeutic value. It helps us cope with our distrust and fear of great corporate size. The country seems to have a need for such therapy in a way that nations with a longer history of strong centralized government do not. Then, too, it would be the height of arrogance for an economist, by remonstrance or innuendo, to chide Congressmen and judges for failing to accept immediately truths that it took his trade the better part of a hundred years to learn. The judicial economics that Robert Bork treats with such scorn is, after all, the blue-ribbon opinion in economics of a generation back.

2.

Romance and Realism in Antitrust Policy

FOR MANY years advocates of antitrust complained that too often government lawyers won the decisions while defendants won the decrees. In their opinions federal judges were prepared to condemn "monopoly" in forceful, even extravagant, language, but were not prepared to follow up with meaningful remedies. Walter Adams once wrote bitterly of the "pyrrhic victories" of antitrust.

Every economist somewhere in his training learns, or should learn, that in an organized capital market, economic rents, including monopoly rents, will be capitalized as soon as they become common knowledge. With the passing of time, such rents will be bought by people who had nothing to do with their creation and who can expect no more than a normal rate of return on their investment in rent collection. As we noted in chapter 1, a corollary to this truth is that the only people who benefit from the creation of a monopoly are those who get in on the ground floor (and their heirs). A second corollary, of course, is that the costs of eliminating monopoly power will fall upon latecomers.

As I learned about the operation of courts and legislatures in this country, it became clear to me that most were extremely reluctant, most of the

Reprinted from *The Journal Political Economy* (April 1955), vol. 63, no. 2.

time, to impose real, measurable, losses on workers and stockholders in order to pursue the ill-defined efficiency goals that enthusiasts set for antitrust. Growing older, I came to regard this reluctance as positively humane and reassuring. This article was written in order to show how this reluctance affects the choice of remedies in antitrust enforcement, especially when the government seeks dissolution or divestiture.

The Fate of the "New" Sherman Act

NEARLY EIGHTEEN years have passed since the Justice Department began the first of the cases that are generally taken to have produced the "new" Sherman Act. For a time in the middle '40s, judicial opinion reflecting the "monopoly is sin" bias of the Temporary National Economic Committee investigations was hailed in some circles as evidence that the venerable statute had finally been transformed into a "positive instrument of progress." Most students of the antitrust scene, however, preferred to reserve judgment pending final disposition of the important cases, for it is a commonplace in antitrust work that the government wins the opinions and the defendants win the decrees. Too often in the past, hopes for a trust-busting program had foundered and sunk on the reluctance of the courts to disturb established corporate structures.

By now it is clear that this caution was fully justified, notwithstanding the efforts of the Justice Department to follow up its legal victories[1] with a radical application of dissolution and divestiture.[2] Even the most cursory look at the results achieved by the "big" cases decided, compromised, or

[1]By my count—probably incomplete—from the Trade Regulation Reports of the Commerce Clearing House, the government has sought some rearrangement of corporate structure in no less than 44 civil suits filed between December 1936, and August 1954.

Among the larger defendants are (or were) Aluminum Corporation of America, Atlantic and Pacific Tea, Pullman, Du Pont, Paramount, Loew's, RKO, Twentieth Century-Fox, Warner Brothers, National Lead, General Electric, Swift, Wilson, Armour, Cudahy, American Telephone and Telegraph, Pan American Airways, United Shoe Machinery, Timken Roller Bearing, Borden's, Proctor and Gamble, Colgate-Palmolive Lever Brothers, Celanese Corporation, International Business Machines, Standard Oil of California, Columbia Gas and Electric, Minnesota Mining and Manufacturing, Pittsburgh Crushed Steel, and United States Rubber.

[2]For a discussion of the mechanics of trust-busting, see the recent symposium, "Divestiture as a Remedy under the Federal Antitrust Laws," *George Washington Law Review*, 19 (December 1950), 119–55. Dissolution is generally taken to mean trust-busting in the literal sense; that is, the carving up of a business organization under single management into a number of smaller independent units. Divestiture denotes the selling-off of certain specified assets— stocks, patents, or plant facilities; thus divestiture, unlike dissolution, leaves the quantity of capital under the control of an offending management substantially unchanged.

abandoned since 1938[3] suffices to establish that the judicial bias in favor of the corporate status quo remains substantially unchanged. Indeed, only the decrees entered in the Pullman[4] and Paramount[5] cases were ambitious enough to merit consideration as possible exceptions to this conclusion.

If one has embraced the comfortable thesis that economic progress is

[3]*United States v. The Pullman Co.*, 53 F. Supp. 908 (1944), 330 U.S. 806 (1947); *United States v. The National Lead Co. et al.*, 332 U.S. 319 (1947); *United States v. Yellow Cab Co.*, 338 U.S. 338 (1949); *United States v. Paramount Pictures et. al.*, 85 F. Supp. 811; *United States v. Aluminum Co. of America*, 44 F. Supp. 97 (1942); 148 F. (2d) 416 (1945); 91 F. Supp. 33 (1950); *United States v. Timken Roller Bearing Co.*, 341 U.S. 593 (1951); *United States v. Columbia Gas & Electric Co. et. al.*, Civil 16, discontinued July, 1953, 1954 Trade Cases 66, 087; *United States v. The New York Great Atlantic and Pacific Tea Co.*, Civil 52–139 D.C. N.Y., 1954 Trade Cases 67, 658; *United States v. United Shoe Machinery Co.*, 110 F. Supp. 295 (1953), 1954 Trade Cases 67, 755; *United States v. Armour & Co. et al.*, Civil 48-C-1351, discontinued March, 1954, 1954 Trade Cases 66, 117.

[4]The Pullman case was a rather irrelevant piece of litigation, as far as the reduction of monopoly power was concerned. The final decree merely divorced a public utility monopoly (the Pullman Company) from its manufacturing subsidiary (Pullman-Standard Car Manufacturing Company) and transferred ownership to the major railroads.

[5]According to one writer, the antitrust action against the major Hollywood producers — Paramount, Loew's, RKO, Warner Brothers, and Twentieth Century-Fox represents "probably the government's greatest economic victory in the 60-year history of antitrust enforcement." Walter Adams, "The Aluminum Case: Legal Victory — Economic Defeat," 41 *Am. Econ. Rev. 915* (1951). In one sense this estimate is undoubtedly correct: in no other case involving a major corporation have the federal attorneys succeeded in gaining court approval for so many of their specific recommendations for relief.

The government secured a decree ending most of the features of film distribution that independent exhibitors have so often denounced as unfair, notably the noncompetitive granting of runs on motion pictures, "unreasonable" clearance, and the studio's setting of minimum admission charges at which its films could be shown. In addition, the studios were compelled to sever connection with their "tied" theater chains (dissolution was elected), and the released circuits were directed to divest themselves of motion picture houses in localities where they were deemed individually or collectively to dominate the market for first-run showings. (At the time of the trial the theater circuits owned by or associated with the Big Five producers paid about one-half of all domestic film rentals.)

In assessing the Paramount decision, however, it should be noted that the case involved mainly considerations of "fair" competition rather than "restraint of trade." For many years, the central fact in film distribution has been the conflict between producer and exhibitor over the type of price discrimination to be practiced in the release of pictures. The producer wishes to insure that anyone who will pay a dollar to see his latest epic today will not be discouraged from doing so by the knowledge that it will reach a cheaper theater within the week; the independent exhibitor commonly has every incentive to reduce admission prices in order to tap the lower-price market that producers prefer to reserve for exploitation at a later date.

Federal intervention in the industry was apparently based on the assumption that the public interest in this conflict lay with the exhibitor. Yet, even on a priori grounds, it is extremely difficult to discern the consequences of alternative policies of discrimination for the rate of motion picture attendance; in practice, such an assessment is quite impossible.

now the unique product of research in the large corporation, the fate of
the new Sherman Act, far from being a matter for concern, is a positive
source of satisfaction. For those of us who still prefer to resolve all doubts
in favor of workable competition whenever the economic advantages of
concentration are not conclusively demonstrated, the defeat of the Antitrust Division would seem to call for a reappraisal of our case.

Legal Fiction as a Source of Confusion

MOST OF our difficulties follow, I believe, from the "fact" that dissolution and divestiture suits are conducted upon a premise which most judges
and laymen really do not accept. Unlike the advocates of strong remedies,
they are not convinced that the exercise of monopoly power which has
been acquired by means neither actionable nor indictable per se violates
the law to an extent justifying its elimination without a sympathetic attention to the position of workers and stockholders whose interests may
be adversely affected by trust-busting.

This view does not regard vested interests in monopoly as bona fide
property rights merely by virtue of their established character. But it does
assume, however inarticulately, that possible public gains must be weighed
against possible private losses and that, the more problematical the public
benefit, the greater the proper conservative bias in favor of private claims.[6]
Thus, it is one thing for the reasonable judge to order the termination of
profitable leasing arrangements to the end that a secondhand market for
shoemaking machinery may hasten the introduction of new equipment; it
is quite another for him to transform a going concern into three smaller

---

[6]For reasons noted later in this paper, judges cannot openly acknowledge that antitrust decrees
are framed after a weighing of public gains against private losses. However, in the most
recent suit involving the United Shoe Machinery Company (110 F. Supp. 295 [D. Mass.
1953]) Judge Wyzanski, in an admirable opinion, came surprisingly close to stating the "true"
case for judicial conservatism. After finding the defendant guilty, he refused the government's
request for the dissolution of the company into three small units, arguing in part:

> In the anti-trust field the courts have been accorded, by common consent, an authority
> they have in no other branch of enacted law. Indeed, the only comparable examples
> of the power of judges is the economic role they formerly exercised under the Four-
> teenth Amendment, and the role they now exercise in the area of civil liberties. They
> would not have been given, or allowed to keep, such authority in the anti-trust field,
> and they would not so freely have altered from time to time the interpretation of its
> substantive provisions, if courts were in the habit of proceeding with the surgical
> ruthlessness that might commend itself to those seeking absolute assurance that there
> will be workable competition, and to those aiming at immediate realization of the
> social, political, and economic advantages of dispersal of power.

units on the hope that consumers will benefit in ways that the Antitrust Division cannot spell out in concrete terms.

Friends of the Antitrust Division may object that possession of monopoly power alone has never constituted a violation of the Sherman Act; that the courts have always required a showing of power over price plus something more—though admittedly the something more is none too clear. Occasionally (notably in the Alcoa case), the courts have appeared to employ a test for unlawful monopolization that would have satisfied Frank Albert Fetter himself. Nevertheless, it is true that they have generally held back from accepting the economist's definition of monopoly as the touchstone of policy. The history of antitrust litigation, however, may fairly be viewed as a struggle over how much importance is to be accorded to economics in the legal definition of monopoly; that is, as an attempt to strengthen the modest safeguards conferred upon competition by the common law.

In 1890, the position of monopoly power at common law was clear enough. "Unreasonably" restrictive agreements among business rivals for the purpose of inhibiting competition were not enforceable at law or equity; but merchants need not fear indictment or civil liability so long as their actions did not violate the ordinary criminal or civil codes.[7] For example, the deliberate use of below-cost pricing to eliminate competition did not expose one to legal penalties so long as it was "rational" business behavior and not intended to gratify a sadistic desire to humble a fellow human beyond the requirements of profit maximization.[8]

Since the coming of the Sherman Act, departures from the common law treatment of monopoly have followed two main lines. On the one hand, the courts have come to treat the elimination of competition by certain methods as so highly suspect that their illegality is virtually presumed. Thus, one may no longer dispose of a troublesome rival by purchasing his facilities at an inordinately high price or force him to terms by pricing below short-run average cost; nor, of course, may one contract with him to share the market or observe fair prices.

On the other hand, the courts have held that the "totality" of the defendant's conduct may be examined in order to determine whether his pol-

---

[7]For a thorough examination of the treatment of trade restraints at common law see J. C. Peppin, "Price-Fixing Agreements under the Sherman Antitrust Law," 28 *Cal. L. Rev.* 297, 667 (1940).

[8]The classic statement of the common law's denial of relief to the victims of what is now called "predatory" competition is the House of Lords' opinion in *Mogul Steamship Co. v. McGregor, Gow & Co.*, A.C. 25 (1892). For a reiteration of this view by an American state court, see *Bohn Manufacturing Co. v. Hollis,* 55 N.W. 1119 (1893).

icies reveal an unlawful "intent" to secure or preserve monopoly power. So far as I know, the courts have never ruled that a firm may not protect itself against the incursion of rivals by producing the better mousetrap or reducing production costs on the existing model. But neither have the courts unambiguously declared that economies of scale in production or research constitute the only valid reasons for permitting the domination of an important industry by a single firm or a handful of firms.[9]

A number of early decisions before the advent of the rule of reason, especially *Northern Securities Co. v. United States*,[10] came close to equating unlawful monopoly with power over price. Since 1940, the courts have seemingly indicated a willingness to jettison the reasonableness test. In the Big Three tobacco case,[11] the Supreme Court implied that unlawful conspiracy could be inferred from parallel action even in the absence of evidence showing overt collusion. In the Alcoa case,[12] Learned Hand's remarkable opinion seemed to convey that, no matter how carefully the defendant has comported himself, the law is violated when he (1) controls too great a fraction of the industry's output and (2) enjoys a size and power that have the effect of frightening off potential rivals. If these two decisions could be taken at their face value—a pitfall to be avoided in the study of antitrust law—Professor Galbraith's "preposterous" conclusion would seem to follow: the very fabric of American capitalism is indeed illegal.

As to the present state of antitrust policy, four observations may be ventured. First, if the court does not accept some version of the textbook definition of monopoly, it must necessarily work with the good-trust/bad-trust dichotomy. This classification is perhaps useful in deciding whether a particular firm should be allowed to strengthen its position by acquiring rivals or important patents. It may also serve to discourage business expansion by particularly antisocial means, notably trade wars. But the reasonableness test leaves the major corporations invulnerable to dissolution or divestiture so long as they forego the cruder methods of dampening competition.

Second, even if the court employs a test for unlawful monopoly more acceptable to most economists, it does not follow that severer remedies will find favor; the court may prove to have some rather surprising notions of what must be done in order to restore "competitive" conditions.

Third, regardless of the legal definition of monopoly implied, the pos-

[9]For perhaps the closest approximation to such a declaration, see Judge Wyzanski's opinion in the United Shoe Machinery case.
[10]193 U.S. 197 (1904).
[11]*American Tobacco Co. v. United States*, 328 U.S. 781 (1946).
[12]148 F. 2d 416 (1945).

sibility that the elimination of power over price may injure the fortunes of innocent parties is seldom explicitly explored in antitrust suits. It is the "company" that is charged with violating the antitrust laws. If the company has unlawfully suppressed competition in the past (in the Pullman case, company records from the 1870s were accepted in evidence), the court is clearly obliged to prescribe action designed to restore competitive conditions.[13] Enforcement of the law cannot be suspended on the plea that the company will suffer if forced to disgorge its ill-gotten gains.[14] Since the corporation is a fictitious person, during the trial the court is under no obligation to take cognizance of the obvious; namely, that the beneficiaries of any successful "attempt to monopolize" are those stockholders, workers, and executives who realized capital gains or higher incomes as a consequence of unlawful business aggrandizement.[15] When the corporation's

[13]In the recently abandoned dissolution suit against the major meat-packers, however, the court failed to play the game. The Attorney General felt compelled to throw in his hand when the court refused to admit evidence relating to the nefarious deeds of the defendants done before 1930 (1954 Trade Cases, 66, 117).

[14]As early as 1913 in *United States v. The Union Pacific Railroad*, 226 U.S. 470, the Supreme Court, in ordering the defendant to dispose of its controlling stock interest in the Southern Pacific Railroad, rejected a plea that the manner of divestiture would work a hardship on the stockholders of the Union Pacific. "So far as is constant with this purpose [forbidding combinations in restraint of trade] a court of equity dealing with such combinations should conserve the property interests involved, but never in such ways as to sacrifice the object and purpose of the statute." (Not that there was much danger in this case that divestiture would destroy monopoly power capitalized in security prices; the two railroads were potential competitors for only a small percentage of their respective volumes of traffic.)

[15]Proponents of a strong antitrust policy often seem to imply that employees have no stake in their employer's power over price. A layman noting the market position of Ford, Chrysler, and General Motors, and the wage scale of automobile workers, may, perhaps, instinctively feel otherwise. In fact, the former view rests upon two tyrannies of abstraction:

1. If a purely competitive labor market is assumed, the wage rate is "given" to the employer, and he presumably has no reason to share any monopoly gains with his workers.
2. If the employer operates in an imperfect labor market, he enjoys monopsony power, so that any exercise of his power over price in the products market necessarily depresses the wage scale and hence is inimical to the interest of his workers.

We need not dwell on the imperfections of the labor market or on the fact that most firms that figure in antitrust suits have entered into collective-bargaining agreements. Only the monopsony effect of restrictive practices is relevant to policy. Unfortunately, the recognition of monopsony has lately served to obscure the intuitively more obvious truth that, if company earnings increase by virtue of monopoly power, the employer is, for this reason alone, more vulnerable to union pressures. He is likely to consent to a higher wage scale, (1) because he can afford it, and (2) because he stands to suffer a greater loss from strike action if he does not. The vulnerability of monopolists to employee pressures is probably what some writers mean when they hold that monopoly may raise wage rates by increasing the value of the marginal product of labor. This product, however, is not really relevant to the setting of the wage rate or the amount of labor taken. If the employer has a free hand in varying

monopoly power antedates the antitrust suit by more than a few years, the presumption is that most persons currently dependent upon the corporation for an income have not materially profited from its exercise.

Finally, although the interests of these parties cannot openly be pleaded to stop the ending of unlawful monopoly, they nevertheless influence the framing of decrees. The Antitrust Division now finds it fairly easy to convince the courts that the activities of a major firm in some sense "unlawfully" restrain competition; but, unless the company officers have committed acts that blatantly offend against acknowledged canons of decency, the fiction that stockholders and workers have no legitimate stake in corporate power over price will seldom suffice to persuade the courts to follow through with the logical remedies.

The Limitations of Painless Trust-Busting

DEFENDERS OF trust-busting will probably object that our preoccupation with its possible effects on the fortunes of innocent parties is quite unnecessary; that the dangers to the interest of workers and stockholders in the plans for corporate reorganizations put forward by the Justice Department are much exaggerated;[16] and that, in fact, a dissolution or divestiture decree has not yet discernibly injured owners or employees in a dismembered concern. I cannot believe that writers who give this assurance perceive its implications. For if a court order directing dissolution or divestiture does not hurt workers and stockholders, only the following

---

the factor combination, he will attempt to equate the marginal revenue product of labor with the marginal cost of labor; and the achievement of monopoly, on a ceteris paribus assumption, always lowers the marginal revenue product of labor. If the employer does not have a free hand in varying the factor combination, he must make the best adjustment open to him. In fine, if monopoly power increases, the firm will always prefer a lower wage bill and accept a higher one.

With the passing of time, any wage increase wrung from monopoly earnings is likely to cause some reduction of employment; capital is substituted for labor in the factor combination, and employer attrition whittles away the featherbedding made possible by such profits. In practice, however, employment in plants where unions have secured wage increases or light work loads is seldom contracted by firing people. Rather, the firm that finds itself with a marginal revenue product for labor that is below the wage rate or below the marginal revenue product of capital corrects this situation by failing to make good the normal wastage of manpower through resignation, death, and retirement. Organized employees who are in on the ground floor when monopoly power is gained by their employers are, I believe, most unlikely to fail to benefit from its exercise.

[16]E.g., Dirlam and Kahn have given this assurance with respect to the government's recently abandoned plan to dissolve the Atlantic and Pacific Tea Company into seven regional chains without manufacturing subsidiaries or a central buying agency (see "Integration and Dissolution of the A & P Company," 29 *Indiana L.J.* 1 (1953).

inferences are possible: (1) the company had no appreciable monopoly power in the first place; (2) the company had previously refrained from making the most profitable use of whatever monopoly power it did possess (i.e., the company was a "good" trust); (3) monopoly power residing in the company was not disturbed by dissolution or divestiture; (4) the unlawful power over price has merely been bequeathed or sold to other corporate units; (5) the fall in income sustained by the company as a consequence of its loss of monopoly power was offset by a fortunate development or concatenation of circumstances unrelated to the antitrust suit—for example, a fall in the cost of raw materials, an increased demand for the firm's output, tax relief, or profitable innovation; or the company may have emerged unscathed from its dissection through luck or good management or any combination of the two; and (6) some monopoly power was eliminated by dissolution or divestiture, but such power had previously rested upon so precarious a foundation that it had never been capitalized into appreciably higher security prices or incorporated into established employee expectations.[17]

Hence, when proponents of trust-busting contend that their measures will reduce monopoly power without inflicting a financial loss on hapless stockholders and employees, we can only conclude that they (1) are mistaken, (2) are employing a definition of monopoly power which an economist cannot accept, or (3) are deliberately eschewing attacks on the more formidable enclaves of monopoly power in the economy. And if capitalized monopoly is the target, their proposals must be rejected as resting upon a premise that is logically untenable. Not only does the destruction of monopoly power entail the imposition of a financial loss upon hapless parties, but the magnitude of the loss is the measure of "monopoly" eliminated.

In view of the obvious limitations of the legal fiction that makes the present employees and stockholders of a corporation responsible for the unlawful policies of past managements, one may doubt whether the courts would consent to impose harsh remedies even if it were clear that monopoly power could be touched in no other way. In fact, the need for the calculated doing of damage to property values is never made apparent in

---

[17]One critic has suggested that there remains a further possibility for painless trust-busting —the rapidly growing industry. But, strictly speaking, this possibility must be ruled out, since, in a well-organized capital market, growth prospects are presumably capitalized. Nevertheless, it is probably true that dissolution and divestiture are most likely to be ordered in the case of expanding industries. The contribution of a moderate decree to the already substantial uncertainty surrounding the future earnings of firms so situated is so problematical that it is more easily ignored by the courts.

an antitrust case. On the contrary, federal attorneys, as a matter of trial technique, resolutely deny that their requests for relief will adversely affect the interests of workers and stockholders. Hence, they are unable to prevent the defendant from suggesting to the judge that, if his decree should harm these groups, ipso facto he will have wantonly destroyed the efficiency of a going concern. Actually, the severity of what the courts regard as a "harsh" decree is much more likely to relate to the vagaries and imperfections of the capital market than to any contemplated destruction of monopoly power.[18] Thus, when stock divestiture is ordered, the investor is normally allowed to retain ownership until a "fair" price obtains for his securities—provided voting rights are surrendered to an acceptable trustee. The probable consequences of trust-busting for employee fortunes is a better index of how it promises to affect the firm's power over price; and our tacit assumption that workers are, so to speak, usually disinterested spectators in an antitrust action involving their employer is perhaps the most telling evidence that we do not really expect a decree that will seriously disturb monopoly power.

In fact, once control over price has been capitalized into the value of securities owned by Johnny-come-latelies or incorporated into wage scales, it is, for all practical purposes, safe from judicial attack. Thus, so far as the reduction of monopoly power is concerned, there are only two situations in which trust-busting is worth the trouble and expense of extended litigation.

The first, of course, is where any financial loss will fall upon the persons who have engineered the unlawful suppression of competition. Judges must ever affirm that a court of equity imposes no penalties for past conduct; but, as one would expect, the most severe decrees involving dissolution and divestiture have been returned against companies whose major stockholders have been personally responsible for the castigated policies of their firms.[19] Unfortunately, the separation of legal ownership and effective control

---

[18]A recent case in point is *United States v. Timken Roller Bearing Co.,* 341 U.S. 593 (1951), where the Supreme Court refused to uphold the provision of the lower court decree directing the American company to dispose of its one-third stock interest in a British firm manufacturing similar products. The Supreme Court was apparently influenced by the knowledge that currency controls would have prevented Timken from readily transferring the proceeds of divestiture out of the United Kingdom, and hence increased the danger that Timken might have taken a capital loss in changing its portfolio (see Walter Adams, "Dissolution, Divorcement, Divestiture: The Pyrrhic Victories of Antitrust," 27 *Indiana L. J.* 1 (1951).

[19]Thus, the government's four earliest successes all involved a check to the ambitions of major stockholders who had received much unfavorable publicity: Edward Harriman, J. P. Morgan, and James J. Hill in the Northern Securities case (1904), 193 U.S. 197; James B. Duke in the American Tobacco Company case (1911), 221 U.S. 106, 191 Fed. 371; John D. Rockefeller

in most large and medium-sized corporations is now so complete that the government has not much opportunity to employ trust-busting as a sub rosa punishment.[20]

As a second possibility, a dissolution or divestiture suit can be prosecuted with some prospect of success when the target is monopoly power which cannot be capitalized; that is, when it is inseparably bound up with the acumen or charisma of particular individuals. In this circumstance, trust-busting can presumably contribute to freer markets by curbing the power and influence of the objectionable entrepreneurs—by forcing the withdrawal of a Duke or a Rockefeller. In short, meaningful antimonopoly remedies can be anticipated only when it is possible for judges to "personalize" the issues, which is to say that until the courts can bring themselves to impose decrees that seriously menace the interests of innocent parties, the Sherman Act can never serve as an instrument to further anyone's program for laissez faire.

The Case for Conservatism

THE LIBERTARIAN of the Fetter-Simons persuasion would therefore seem to have a choice of three courses of action. He can return undaunted to the battle in the hope that he may yet persuade the courts that dissolution and divestiture designed to injure hapless workers and stockholders falls

---

in the Standard Oil case (1911), 221 U.S. 1; and Harriman again in the Union Pacific case (1912), 226 U.S. 61.

One suspects that the recent severe use of divestiture (not yet completed) against the number of independent film exhibitors who had energetically collected small-town theaters in the 1920s and 1930s was based in part on the court's knowledge that most of the original promoters were still active in their respective firms. *United States v. Schine Chain Theaters*, 334 U.S. 110 [1948]; *United States v. Crescent Amusement Company*, 323 U.S. 173 [1944]; *United States v. Griffith Amusement Co.*, 334 U.S. 100 [1948].

[20]Judging from the manner in which divestiture has been employed over the years, one might plausibly infer that a major object of antitrust policy is the substitution of management control for owner control in the large corporation. Court decrees have hastened this process in the Standard Oil companies, the tobacco companies that were originally a part of the Duke empire (American, Liggett and Myers, Reynolds, P. Lorillard, and British-American) and, most recently, the Aluminium Company Limited of Canada. If the government ever succeeds in divesting the Du Pont Company of its stock in General Motors and United States Rubber and dissolving the holding companies to which the Du Pont family have transferred their shares in the chemical concern, the principal beneficiaries will be the salaried top managements of the three industrial giants.

The Antitrust Division obviously has no interest in promoting management control. If many antitrust suits contribute to this end, it is only because the shuffling of stock certificates that accompanies the dissolution or divestiture decree presents the managers with control of the company's proxy machine.

within the domain of "reasonable" behavior. But, of course, the libertarian cannot elect this alternative unless he has first convinced himself that failure to pursue an aggressive free-market policy will untimately place the country in dire jeopardy. (Some police state variety of state socialism is generally made the end of the road for big-business capitalism by the friends of trust-busting.) For better or worse, most of us have not the confidence in our own prescience that this course requires.

As a second possibility, the libertarian can discard the legalistic approach to antitrust problems and acknowledge monopoly power as a bona fide property right, which the state may not destroy without paying compensation. Thus, if the public interest is thought to require dissolution in the aluminum industry, the assets of the member firms could be acquired at their monopoly valuation, and new firms organized and sold for what they will bring as competitive units. To the extent that workers have managed to obtain part of the fruits of the industry's power over price, they too must be guaranteed against any loss of income sustained as a consequence of the compulsory reorganization.

The administrative difficulties that would accompany any effort to carry out a compensated elimination of monopoly require no comment, and they probably explain why it is never seriously proposed. But then, if one accepts the reduction of monopoly power as a goal justifying resort to such a program, it is only a short step to the view that the public's great stake in trust-busting makes indemnification unnecessary.

Finally, the libertarian can come to terms with his world by recognizing that dissolution and divestiture on the scale requested by the Antitrust Division is simply not palatable to most legislators and judges. He will recognize that, at this late date, the large corporation is not to be destroyed by a frontal assault, however much one may regret that it was allowed to entrench itself in the first place. And for transforming competition among the giant few into some more acceptable variety, he will place his hopes in unspectacular Fabian tactics—the blocking of doubtful mergers, close scrutiny of the awarding of government contracts and the disposition of surplus federal property, curtailment of the patent privilege, and the harassment of trade associations. Whether defensive measures of this sort will suffice to achieve the libertarian goal is, of course, as yet an open question.[21]

---

[21]For an optimistic statement of the case for defensive strategy, see the testimony of Professor Walter Adams in *Hearings Before the Subcommittee on Study of Monopoly Power of the Committee on the Judiciary, House of Representatives* (81st Cong., 1st sess.), pp. 335–60. While regretting the coolness of the courts toward trust-busting, Adams feels that monopoly will gradually wither away if new industries can be kept free of patent abuses, federal favoritism, and, especially, mergers.

In summary, it is the burden of this paper that the new Sherman Act is rapidly becoming indistinguishable from the old; that this result was "inevitable," given the judicial reluctance to disturb private rights in the interest of promoting nebulous public goals; that in most antitrust cases this conservatism is both understandable and commendable; and that, on balance, ambitious attempts at trust-busting probably do the aims of the Antitrust Division more harm than good. At best, dissolution and divestiture suits tie up the agency's limited means in lengthy battles which will probably be lost. At worst, the occasional securing of a dismembering decree which does not touch monopoly power may delude the friends of antitrust policy into thinking that they are progressing in the right direction.

A recent study by Professor Fred Weston, however, suggests that monopoly power may not be so vulnerable to a ban on mergers as Adams believes (*The Role of Mergers in the Growth of Large Firms* [1953]). Weston found that in the 74 firms whose expansion was studied for the period 1895–1910 through 1948, mergers accounted for no more than one-third of the aggregate increase in assets. But, as he points out, in some industries, notably steel, ammunition, and cement, over one-half of corporate growth can be traced to mergers. For a detailed discussion of Weston's study see G. Warren Nutter, "Growth by Merger," 49 *J. Am. Stat. Ass'n.,* 448 (1954).

3.

Imperfect Competition No Bar to Efficient Production

Abstract reasonings as to the effects of the economies in production, which an individual firm gets from an increase of its output are apt to be misleading, not only in detail, but even in their general effect.

—Alfred Marshall

*W*HEN I first began the study of economics I was early introduced to the propositions that the main objection to monopoly and monopolistic and/or imperfect competition was not that they led to excess profits (or economic rents, as I later learned to call them) but that they imposed a welfare loss by misallocating resources; and that in the case of monopolistic and/or imperfect competition, resource misallocation took the form of the creation of excess capacity. It was—and, for that matter, still is—widely believed that the truth of these propositions had been conclusively demonstrated by the early work of Joan Robinson and Edward Chamberlin.

Later in my studies, I was to learn that there were economists who questioned whether "free" or, at any rate easy, entry under conditions of less than perfect competition must necessarily lead to excess capacity. For they were aware that an industry characterized by excess capacity could be "rationalized" by consolidation into a multiplant firm or a profit-sharing cartel. (Even Robinson knew about industrial rationalization schemes.) These early critics of the "excess capacity theorem" could point out that an equilibrium with excess capacity was unstable, but they were largely

Reprinted from *The Journal of Political Economy* (1958), vol. 66, no. 24.

ignored, especially by textbook writers, because they could not prove either the existence or impossibility of equilibrium when perfect competition was not assumed.

From this distance in time, I cannot be sure how much my own thinking about the excess capacity problem owed to these early skeptics, notably Don Patinkin and Morris Copeland. (Anyone who reads the industrial organization literature or business history soon meets the concept of rationalization—there is nothing esoteric about it.) I am sure that the central idea for this article—that equilibrium involves rationalization plus the use of limit pricing—came to me after reading fairly widely in the investigations of the so-called trust movement that swept the American economy in the 1890s and early 1900s. Thus, John D. Rockefeller systematically eliminated excess capacity in the oil industry through the reorganizations that followed his mergers and takeovers. Through costly experience, he learned the advisability of using limit pricing to prevent the re-entry of competitors whom he had already bought out.

A fair question is why this article treats the problem of achieving stable equilibrium under conditions of imperfect competition in the context of spatial competition. The answer is that I was still under the influence of Edward Chamberlin and hence could not assume away the selling expenses to which he attached so much importance and handled so badly. (A sophisticated treatment of selling expenses requires resort to mathematics and, even by the standards in economics of sixty years ago, Chamberlin was a limited mathematician.) To make the problem tractable, I had to find a total revenue function that was not affected by outlays on transportation or advertising. This need was satisfied by the assumption of a price elasticity of demand that was unitary in all markets.

Over the years this article attracted a select but quite small readership. However, its central idea—even in its later and simplified formulations—never passed into mainstream price theory as embalmed in the textbooks of economic theory—basic, intermediate, and advanced. There the geometry of Robinson and Chamberlin (or its mathematical formulation) still rules supreme. The reason, let us hope, is because Robinson and Chamberlin are easier to teach and time is limited. Having introduced the class to perfect competition, it is only necessary for the instructor to give the firm's horizontal demand curve a downward tilt in order to proceed directly to the case of imperfect competition—including the fashionable subcase of oligopoly. One does not like to contemplate the possibility that textbook authors do not know about industrial rationalization and limit pricing.

The approach of this article, of course, is not the only one for dealing with the imperfections and misleading policy implications of Robinson and Chamberlin. Milton Friedman once proposed to deal with them by confining the study of markets to the polar cases of perfect competition and monopoly. This he did on the assumption that nothing was to be gained in predictability by bringing in anything else. William Baumol has introduced the device of a contestable market which, being (almost) always efficient, eliminates the excess capacity problem. These alternative treatments have the advantage of greater simplicity. But in defense of the more cumbersome approach to imperfect competition outlined below, I would cite the wisdom attributed to Alfred Einstein: "Things should be made as simple as possible but no simpler." In the study of real world markets too much is lost if the effects of industrial rationalization and limit pricing are assumed away. They are important and permanent features of competition as most of us understand the term.

Limitations of Geometry Are a Source of Confusion

THIS ARTICLE examines a proposition now developed in most textbook treatments of imperfect or monopolistic competition. The proposition is that, if producers enjoy free entry into imperfect markets, a no-profit/no-loss equilibrium will be reached in which each firm is of less than optimum size. That is, not only is the industry's equilibrium output too small when judged by almost any welfare criteria but production is technically inefficient in the sense that, if the industry's organization were rationalized, the equilibrium output itself could be produced more cheaply by distributing it among fewer and larger producing units.[1]

This thesis is generally expounded with the aid of conventional graphical analysis. The imperfect competitor is given a U-shaped curve depicting total average cost and a negatively sloped demand curve (figure 3.1). And, since the demand curve cannot be tangent to the U-shape cost curve save at a point where the latter is falling, the inefficiency of the firm in a no-profit/no-loss equilibrium in imperfect competition is held to follow pari passu. "The impossibility of production under the most efficient conditions is settled once and for all by the shape of the demand curve."[2]

The use of geometry to analyze price-making in imperfectly competi-

---

[1]See, for example, Edward Chamberlin, *The Theory of Monopolistic Competition,* 2d ed. (1936), pp. 104–09; Joan Robinson, *The Economics of Imperfect Competition* (1933), pp. 96–97; M. W. Reder, *The Theory of Welfare Economics* (1947), pp. 54–55; J. E. Meade, *Economic Analysis and Policy* (1936), pp. 154–55; W. J. Baumol and L. V. Chandler, *Economic Processes and Policies* (1954), pp. 428–29; and K. E. Boulding, *Economic Analysis,* 3rd ed. (1955), pp. 628–30.
[2]Chamberlin, p. 98.

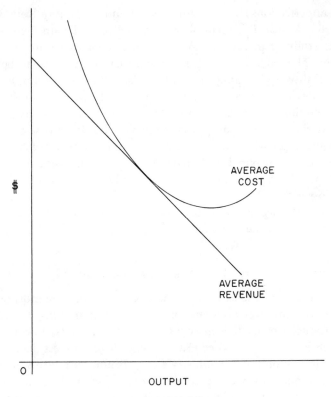

FIGURE 3.1

tive markets, however, is a very doubtful expedient. If the market is made imperfect by the existence of selling costs and transport expenses, the conventional graphical analysis has no validity. It depicts cost and revenue on the assumption that each is solely a function of the rate of output; yet any change in marketing outlay will change the total average cost of any output and will probably change the firm's collection of demand curves as well. This commonplace truth—and its implications for economic theory—was explicitly recognized by Sraffa[3] and Harrod[4] during the increasing returns controversy of the late '20s and early '30s. In the influential treatises of Chamberlin and Mrs. Robinson, however, the complications of transport and selling costs are brushed aside, and the use of geometry is retained. Most later writers have followed this lead.

[3]"The Laws of Returns under Competitive Conditions," 36 *Econ. J.* 535 (1926).
[4]"The Laws of Decreasing Costs," 41 *Econ J.* 567 (1931).

Now, if the graphical analysis is insisted upon, there would seem to be three legitimate ways of dealing with marketing expenses.

1. The U-shape cost curve can be made to stand for average manufacturing ("production") cost only, while the firm's demand curve can be drawn on the assumption that it depicts the maximum revenue that can be realized from any quantity of output after all marketing costs have been deducted. If this approach is favored, nothing can be said about the optimum size of the firm, since the diagram gives no information about total average cost. But a priori it is improbable that total average cost would be minimized by having the firm operate at the rate of output at which average manufacturing cost is lowest.

2. Average cost and revenue curves can be drawn on the premise that they describe the most profitable—or least unprofitable—combination of production, selling, and transport costs that obtain for each rate of output.[5] If this approach is chosen, it does not follow that the firm achieves a no-profit/no-loss equilibrium where total average cost is falling. Such an equilibrium would be possible where both total average revenue and total average cost were rising, but total average cost was rising faster. No inferences about efficiency could be drawn from an analysis based upon these "true" total cost and revenue curves. For example, a true decreasing average cost for the equilibrium firm would merely signify that, *if* it were compelled to produce and market an additional unit of product, the ensuing loss would be minimized by a relatively small increase in total selling and transport costs.

3. The study of imperfect competition can proceed on Mrs. Robinson's assumption that selling and transport costs have nothing to do with the imperfection; that is, these inconvenient expenses can be assumed away.[6] This popular approach, alas, invites error! The only other source of market imperfection is the existence of overhead manufacturing costs in the firm which, when joined to limited demand, make it impossible for the industry to support the number of firms needed for impersonal price making.

---

[5] No one seems ever to have drawn cost and revenue curves on this assumption. The method of construction that it implies, however, was obliquely suggested by Harrod many years ago (ibid., p. 571).

[6] In *The Economies of Imperfect Competition,* transport and selling costs are assumed away. In an earlier article, Mrs. Robinson applied the graphical analysis to a case where the "imperfection of the market is due to differential transport costs" ("Imperfect Competition and Falling Supply Price," *Econ J.* 544 (1932). The error involved in this application, however, was pointed out in a comment by G. F. Shove, "The Imperfection of the Market: A Further Note," *Econ. J.* 133 (1933).

Product Differentiation and the Alleged Wastes of Imperfect Competition

THE READER may object that any discussion of the alleged wastes of imperfect competition must make some mention of the economic consequences of "product differentiation." I confess to holding the conviction that economists qua economic theorists—as distinct from moral philosophers—have nothing to say about the social disutility of product differentiation.

Suppose that two "functionally identical" ten-ounce bottles of fluid sell for different prices while standing side by side. (The "functional identity" has been established by an "independent body composed of reputable chemists, psychologists, and economists.") What inferences are possible?

Clearly buyers are (1) uninformed or (2) misinformed. (We assume that our independent body of experts did not err in its findings). If buyers are deceived by advertising, no doubt the advertisers should be ashamed of themselves. No doubt, also, the resources employed to perpetrate the deception are, in a very real sense, "wasted." But what action, if any, should be taken to suppress "bad" sales promotion depends on many things— and not the least on one's larger political philosophy. If buyers are uninformed because they are not experts, it may pay the state to invest in a program of consumer education. Then, again, it may not. Even consumer education has its cost.

Suppose, however, that the two ten-ounce bottles of fluid that sell side by side for different prices are not functionally identical. Now, so far as I can see, the two bottles "really" are different products. The fact that the difference can be traced to entrepreneurial ingenuity rather than to innate differences in consumer tastes is immaterial. And "real" differences in products raise no analytical difficulties for the economist. Production is not inefficiently organized unless the cost of producing the output of some particular product could be cut. It is the thesis of this paper that there will be no technically inefficient provision of a "product" even though the market is imperfect.

Let me cast a parting stone by submitting that textbook treatments of product differentiation show the danger of mixing one's positive and welfare economics. That some product differentiation is bad is a proposition accepted by most people. Economists would do well to confine their remarks on the subject to the obvious truth that product differentiation is bad to the extent that it represents someone's exploitation of the gullibility and ignorance of his fellow man.

No good purpose is served by attempting to show that "rational" exploitation of consumer "irrationality" leads not only to the production of the wrong commodities in the wrong amounts but to their production in firms of less than optimum size as well. To do this successfully, one would have to show that the exploiters do not know their business; that is, that existing quantities of the wrong products could be produced and marketed more cheaply if production were rationalized. The ineptness of the producers of bad products in victimizing the public has never been demonstrated. If the thesis of this paper is correct, it cannot be demonstrated.

In any event, economists who inveigh against the wastes of product differentiation really do not mean to suggest that the cost of producing the existing quantities of the wrong products could be cut by a state-imposed rationalization scheme. Rather, they would economize resources either by persuading people to want the right goods or by restricting consumer choice to the extent that consumers choose unwisely.

In conclusion, let us be quite dogmatic. The concept of "an industry producing differentiated products" has no place in any economic analysis that takes tastes and resources as "given." If two functionally identical ten-ounce bottles of fluid sell side by side for different prices, they are, for purposes of supply and demand analysis, separate products. And the availability of substitutes for a product is taken into account when a demand function is assigned to it. These observations are not meant to imply that economists should abandon the study of the phenomenon of product differentiation by producers as a substitute for price-cutting. They are only meant to establish that static analysis has no contribution to make to the study of this phenomenon.

Efficiency and Equilibrium in a Market Made Imperfect by a Transport Cost

IF EACH firm in no-profit/no-loss equilibrium operates where total average cost is falling, the industry is, of course, inefficiently conducted. The cost of what it produces could be reduced by concentrating production in fewer, larger, and more fully utilized plants. But, if we assume producer rationality and freedom of contract, no permanent equilibrium has yet been reached. Nor will it be reached until a monopoly has emerged that (1) maintains a rate of output high enough to discourage the entry of new firms and (2) produces this output in the cheapest way. This argument is developed below.

When a temporary no-profit no-loss equilibrium obtains with firms of less than optimum size, it is "as if" total average cost for the industry were falling; and the instability of this market situation (with marketing costs ignored) was demonstrated many years ago by Frank H. Knight.[7] The elimination of firms will continue until the remaining producers are of optimum size or until a monopoly has emerged.

We have seen that a definition of imperfect competition that rules out selling and transport costs has no significance. It is because these marketing outlays check the expansion of output before all manufacturing economies have been realized that we may meaningfully distinguish imperfect competition from monopoly and perfect competition. Let us, therefore, examine the problem of efficient output in imperfect markets on the explicit premise that a marketing cost is present; but, while forswearing the temptations of geometry, let us keep our model as simple as possible. We shall assume:

1. The only marketing expense is a cost of transport from factory to market.
2. Markets are located at equal intervals along an endless road.
3. Each market has the same demand curve; this demand curve has an elasticity of unity at all points.
4. The freight rate is uniform per unit of distance.
5. The rate of output at which average manufacturing cost is minimized in each plant depends upon how the plant is designed, so that the long-run curve of total average manufacturing cost has the traditional envelope shape.
6. A plant can be located in any market along the road.

Let us also in the first instance—and for the purposes of exposition only—assume that the industry is organized by a monopolist legally protected from competition. Since elasticity of demand is unity in all markets, his objective is clear. He must design and locate his plants so as to sell one unit of product in each market at the lowest possible total average delivered cost. It will not profit him to deliver more than one unit of product to each market; the injection of a second unit would merely reduce the price by half and leave the total revenue yielded by the market unchanged. The monopolist knows his production possibilities; hence, the solution of this problem is a simple exercise in calculus.

We can write:

$$t = \text{unit cost of transport between adjoining markets;}$$
$$x = \text{the rate of output per plant;}$$
$$ax^2 + b = \text{total manufacturing cost per plant where } a < 1 < b;$$

[7]"Some Fallacies in the Interpretation of Social Cost," 38 *Q. J. Econ.* 582 (1924).

$r =$ the revenue obtainable in each market subject to the restriction that

$$\frac{r}{\sqrt{b/a}} < (ax^2 + b)/x$$

(As we shall presently note, this restriction is necessary to insure that the whole output of a plant is not sold in the plant's "home" market and all transport costs thereby evaded; $\sqrt{b/a}$ is the output that gives the minimum value of $(ax^2 + b)/x$; and

$xr =$ the revenue obtainable for selling in x different markets.

Total average cost is the sum of average manufacturing cost y and average delivery cost u. Average manufacturing cost is given by

$$y = (ax^2 + b)/x \tag{3.1}$$

Average manufacturing cost is minimized when

$$dy/dx = 0$$

or when

$$x = \sqrt{b/a}$$

The construction of an equation which gives average delivery cost as a function of the rate of output presents a problem, since the average cost of delivering a given quantity of output depends on where it goes. Here, the premise of unitary elasticity of demand in each market comes to our rescue. The monopolist will not sell more than one unit in each market. For one unit of output only there is no transport cost; it can be sold for r in the "home" market. The cost of transporting a unit to one of the two markets located nearest to the home market is t. The total cost of delivering three units to the three most profitable markets is $2t$.

The cost of transporting a unit of product to one of the two nth markets served by a plant is nt; and the total transport cost incurred in marketing x units of output in x different markets is therefore

$$2t + 4t + 6t + \ldots \frac{2(x - 1)t}{2} \tag{3.2}$$

or

$$\frac{x^2 t - t}{4}$$

Average cost of delivery u is given by

$$u = \frac{x^2 t - t}{4x} \tag{3.3}$$

or

$$u = \frac{tx - tx^{-1}}{4} .$$

Average total cost is

$$y + u \tag{3.4}$$

or

$$\left(a + \frac{1}{4}t\right)x + \left(b - \frac{1}{4}t\right)x^{-1}$$

Profit per unit of distance is maximized when the average total cost of selling one unit in every market is minimized; that is, when

$$\frac{d(y + u)}{dx} = 0$$

or when

$$x = \sqrt{\frac{b - \frac{1}{4}t}{a + \frac{1}{4}t}}$$

Average manufacturing cost, as we noted above, is minimized when

$$x = \sqrt{b/a}$$

Consequently, when a transport cost is present, the rate of output which minimizes average total cost is less than the rate of output which minimizes average manufacturing cost; so that the monopolist's equilibrium output is distributed among plants in which average manufacturing cost is falling. Nevertheless, he provides one unit of output to each market in the most efficient manner.

Let us now open the industry—that is, our endless road of many markets—to anyone who wishes to intrude. Suppose, for simplicity's sake, that the entrenched monopolist has a total cost equal to half the maximum revenue obtainable per unit of distance. It follows, given our assumption of unitary elasticity of demand in each market, that an intruder by exactly duplicating the monopolist's effort—that is, by himself selling one unit in every market at the lowest possible cost—could capture half the maximum revenue obtainable per unit of distance. The entry of an intruder on this scale would eliminate profit from the industry but leave the average total cost unchanged. It also follows that the industry is now inefficiently organized, since the monopolist could have cut average total cost by increasing the number of units sold in each market.

We can compute the optimum output per plant when the object is to sell two units in every market. Average manufacturing cost y remains

$$(ax^2 + b)/x$$

We must, however, construct a new equation which will yield u—average delivery cost expressed as a function of output when two units are sold in every market. For two units only, there are no transport costs; they can be sold in the home market. The total cost of transporting two units to one of the two markets located nearest the home market is $2t$. And the total cost of transporting six units in a way that (1) minimizes transport cost while (2) placing two units in every market is $4t$. It follows that the total cost of transporting x units so as to place two units in every market is half the total cost of transporting x units so as to place one unit in every market (see eq. 3.2).

The average cost of transporting two units to every market can now be written:

$$u_2 = \frac{1}{2}\left(\frac{x^2 t - t}{4x}\right) \tag{3.5}$$

or

$$u_2 = \frac{x^2t - t}{8x}$$

When two units are delivered to every market, average total cost is

$$y + u_2 = \frac{ax^2 + b}{x} + \frac{x^2t - t}{8x}$$

or

$$y + u_2 = \left(a + \frac{1}{8}t\right)x + \left(b - \frac{1}{8}t\right)x^{-1}.$$

The average total cost of sending two units to every market is minimized when

$$\frac{d(y + u_2)}{dx} = 0$$

or when[8]

$$x = \sqrt{\frac{b - \frac{1}{8}t}{a + \frac{1}{8}t}}$$

The capitalized value of an industry that sells two units in every market when each plant has an output of

$$\sqrt{\frac{b - \frac{1}{4}t}{a + \frac{1}{4}t}}$$

[8]This expression can, of course, be generalized. The average total cost of selling g units in every market is minimized when

$$x = \sqrt{\left(b - \frac{t}{4g}\right) \Big/ \left(a + \frac{t}{4g}\right)}$$

is less than that of an industry which sells two units in every market by having each plant produce an output of

$$\sqrt{\frac{b - \frac{1}{8}t}{a + \frac{1}{8}t}}.$$

Assuming both rational business behavior and freedom of contract, the original monopolist and the intruder will either combine and rationalize production or sell out to a third party who will do the job.

If free entry into the industry is allowed, the rationalized monopoly must necessarily "overproduce" and sacrifice some part of its profit to insure that a potential rival does not become an actual rival.[9] It only remains for us to show that the monopolist can avail himself of this protection.

Suppose that an exceptionally cautious monopolist were to sacrifice his monopoly profit completely in order to secure a quiet life; that he can do this by selling g units ($g > 1$) in each market; and that he has minimized the average total cost of selling g units in every market. The average total cost of selling g units in every market is minimized by producing

$$\sqrt{\left(b - \frac{t}{4g}\right) \Big/ \left(a + \frac{t}{4g}\right)}$$

units in every plant; and this output is less than the $\sqrt{b/a}$ units needed to minimize average manufacturing cost.

[9]The objection may be raised that, when the rational monopolist is faced with competition, he may react by bribing potential competitors to stay out or by letting them in "up to a point." If the offer of a bribe is accepted, the monopolist is poorer, but the industry rate of output, spatial distribution of output, and average total cost of output are unchanged. This sort of business blackmail is not unknown to patent attorneys. It is, however, excluded by our assumption of free entry—the monopolist will still face aspiring competitors after his monopoly profit has been paid out in Danegeld.

There is no reason why a rational monopolist should not yield to competitors so long as the profit sacrificed by letting them in is no greater than the profit that must be lost by the overproduction necessary to keep them out. It is of no consequence to him that the first course of action has a social cost, because it leads to output being distributed among plants of less than optimum size. But, for the reasons noted above, this inefficiency cannot persist. A single firm producing a given output efficiently is always worth more than two firms producing the same output inefficiently; hence, it will pay somebody to acquire the inefficient firms at their capitalized value and reap a capital gain by rationalizing their production.

When the monopolist adopts the extreme course of foregoing all profit while producing efficiently, the rational intruder is effectively barred from entering the market. He cannot get an average total cost as low as the monopolist's without himself selling *g* units in every market; his average total cost exceeds the monopolist's average total cost and, hence, average revenue. When a rationalized monopoly just breaks even, no intruder can profitably sell in any market. Hence, any spatial distribution of output from the plants of a rationalized monopoly that just suffices to discourage the entry of an intruder will afford the rationalized monopoly some profit.

We might note parenthetically that our industry has decreasing average cost only so long as some part of a plant's output is sold beyond the market in which the plant is located—so long, that is, as a transport cost is incurred. If the transport cost is made zero, our endless road of many markets is pari passu transformed into a perfectly competitive industry; the markets formerly kept separate by the transport cost disappear into one big market, and the demand for the output of any single plant becomes infinitely elastic. Alternatively, one can retain the postulate of a transport cost but assign a value to *r* so that

$$\frac{r}{\sqrt{b/a}} \gtreqless \frac{ax^2 + b}{x}$$

When this condition holds, a plant can cover its total cost by selling $\sqrt{b/a}$ units—the output which minimizes average manufacturing cost—in the home market. Hence, when it does not pay to transport goods, the industry's output has constant average cost; any additional increment will be provided by increasing the number of plants which produce $\sqrt{b/a}$ units.

In short, the assumptions which permit imperfect competition imply either efficient monopoly or efficient competition. So long as some part of a plant's output is sold beyond its home market, each plant has an exclusive sales territory and produces and distributes its output in the most efficient manner. The fact that a plant could cut average total cost by selling a greater output in its exclusive territory (or changing its spatial distribution of output) is not material. No market will contain more than one plant unless a plant can break even by selling, in that market, an output which minimizes its long-run average manufacturing cost.

Nor is maximum efficiency achieved in our market made imperfect by a transport cost, only because we assume that the industry is dominated by a single monopolist. If each plant is individually owned, the burden of discouraging the entry of new firms is more widely distributed. But each plant owner has a stake in his own particular monopoly, and he can make it unprofitable for anyone to invade his market area by the necessary "overproduction." Having decided upon the rate and distribution of his output, the plant owner will minimize his loss of profit by selecting the location and design of plant that minimizes his average total cost.

Admittedly, an industry composed of many small monopolists would have a coordination problem. Nevertheless, independent firms in our model will either learn to behave "as if" they were the coordinated units of a single monopoly; or they will sell out to a promoter for a price that is greater than the industry's capitalized value as an incompetently managed collection of firms but less than its capitalized value as a rationalized monopoly. If one assumes that production is guided by the prospect of profit—and that this prospect can be intelligently assessed and freely pursued—an equilibrium peopled by firms of less than optimum size is a contradiction in terms.

It also follows, contrary to the conclusion advanced in most treatments of spatial competition, that free entry cannot eliminate all monopoly profit when a transport cost is the source of market imperfection. The portion of the monopolist's gain that remains after he has cut price low enough to make the entry of newcomers unprofitable is best viewed as a variety of economic rent that accrues to him who first organizes production efficiently.

The Wastes of Imperfect Competition as a Product of Irrationality and Ignorance

HAS THE proposition that imperfect competition produces a no-profit/no-loss equilibrium in which firms are of less than optimum size no validity? The answer, I believe, is that inefficiency may characterize markets made imperfect by transport and selling costs for reasons that have nothing to do with the sources of imperfection.

If an industry is inefficiently conducted, it will always profit the established firms to combine for the purpose of rationalizing production. In practice, rationalization through combination may be extremely difficult to achieve, especially if the industry has considerable excess capacity. Some firms may "irrationally" prefer to retain their autonomy; and, even though the desire to rationalize in the interests of higher profits is universally present, negotiators may lack the requisite skills to bring it off. So long as the excess capacity engendered by inefficiency persists, the construction of larger and more efficient plants may not pay. It is only in a purely competitive industry that the ability of an established inefficient firm to break even is proof positive that an efficient producer can profitably enter the field.

Again, imperfect competition may be associated with inefficiency because established producers and aspiring producers habitually overestimate their prospects and so give the industry an output that could be more cheaply produced if it were planned for in advance. Economic waste of this sort, however, is rooted in investor psychology; and it is more likely to characterize a purely competitive industry where, almost axiomatically, entry is even easier.

We may conclude, therefore, that the textbook demonstration that imperfect competition gives rise to a no-profit/no-loss equilibrium in which firms are of less than optimum size should be discarded. In "static" analysis, the case against a laissez faire policy toward imperfect competition must stand or fall on the possibility of demonstrating that "welfare" would be enhanced by an increase in the output of imperfectly competitive industries.

4.

The Ambiguous Notion of Average Cost

W HAT FOLLOWS is an exercise in basic price theory. While it has no claim to originality, it was one that somebody had to devise and all economists should work through somewhere in their training. Merchants, investors, and renters have known that expected incomes are capitalized into present market values at some rate of interest since, in the fine old legal phrase, the mind of man runneth not to the contrary. Economists who study the shifting and incidence of property taxes have known this truth for at least two hundred years. Nevertheless, a recognition of its implications for "the monopoly problem" has been very slow in coming. Since I was also doing work in capital theory in the 1960s, my own education was speeded up. I could hardly avoid recognizing that, in a world of organized markets, an economic rent will be capitalized whenever it appears.

As the exercise shows, once an economic rent is capitalized into the curve of average total (unit) cost, all firms that operate under conditions of perfect competition will appear to be producing the most efficient output. Firms that operate under condition of imperfect competition will appear to be producing a suboptimal output, that is, one at which average

Reprinted from *The Journal of Industrial Economics* (July 1962), vol. 10, no. 3.

total cost is falling. Therefore, all generalizations about economic welfare based upon cost functions derived from accounting data must be received with suspicion unless the rent component has been explicitly isolated. And models of monopolistic and/or imperfect competition that show free entry eliminating economic rent in equilibrium (as they do in virtually all textbooks) must be treated as flawed. The compounded error, of course, is to use cost data that contains embedded rent to validate an economic model that assumes the elimination of rent.

Since economists are tied to the chariots of policy makers they are often pulled on to new problems before they have resolved—or at any rate, clarified—the old ones. A notable example of the confusion that can result from the failure to tie up loose ends is afforded by treatments of "average cost of production" in textbooks, treatises, and empirical investigations.

Most authors assume that the "efficiency" of a firm is related to the point on its curve of average total cost at which it operates. Not a few authors assume that many firms use average cost plus some markup as, at least, a first approximation in determining price. And innumerable efforts over the years have been devoted to discerning the "real" average cost functions of business firms from accounting data and other information supplied by business men. Since "average cost" is an ambiguous term, albeit one regularly used by economists and businessmen alike, there may be merit in describing a pedagogical device that points up its different meanings and their implications.

In a general way, economists and businessmen have long perceived the undesirability of attaching too much importance to average cost in drawing inferences about the profitability or efficiency of a particular business operation. Older economists resolutely distinguished between "cost" as an expense that must be incurred to secure the service of a productive factor and "rent" as the bonus payment which a productive factor might command over and above this cost. In the United States, government regulatory bodies have declined to allow utility companies, which require deposits from customers, to count these deposits as "capital investment" for rate-making purposes. (In legal theory, utility companies are entitled to charge rates which afford them a fair rate of return on a fair valuation of capital investment). An "everybody knows" that the incomes made possible by contrived scarcities—permits to operate taxicabs, urban land sites zoned for skyscrapers, etc.—can be capitalized in an organized capital market.

Nevertheless, the limitations of the notion of average cost in a business world where the capitalization of expected incomes is continuous and nearly universal are frequently overlooked, particularly in discussions of the welfare costs of imperfect competition. The following simple geometry can, I believe, be employed to make clear the nature of average cost and to expose pitfalls awaiting anyone who uses this concept uncritically.

Assume that one firm receives the sole right to operate taxicabs in its town. Assume further, for the sake of simplicity, that its fixed costs are negligible; and that the difficulties of coordinating cab drivers are such that the unit cost of carrying passengers increases as the number carried rises. This unit cost is both average total cost (ATC) and average variable cost (AVC) in figure 4.1. It therefore implies the marginal cost curve (MC) depicted in figure 4.1. Also shown are the firm's demand curve (P) and its implied marginal revenue curve (MR). Since the firm is a protected monopolist, profit is maximized by equating marginal cost to marginal revenue. This equality is achieved with output *OA* and a price *OD* which gives a "monopoly profit" *EBCD*.

Assume now that the firm which holds the exclusive franchise to operate taxicabs decides to lease it to a latecomer (who is equally efficient at operating taxicabs). The rental charge exacted will, of course, be equal to monopoly profit *EBCD*. The second firm will treat this rental as a fixed cost. The cost and revenue position of the second firm is given by figure

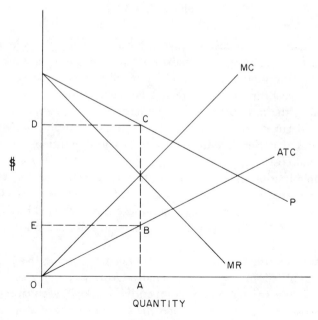

FIGURE 4.1

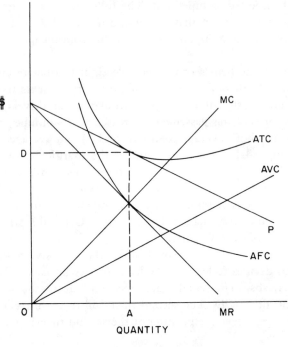

FIGURE 4.2

4.2. Now average total cost and average variable cost are no longer identical; the latecomer appears to make no profit. But not only has the capitalization of monopoly profit into a franchise rental raised the curve of average total cost for the second firm. The shape of this curve has changed. Superficially, the new firm appears to have excess capacity, in the sense that it could cut average total cost by expanding output; whereas figure 3.1 indicates that the first firm operated under conditions of increasing average total cost.

The capitalization of monopoly profit into a fixed cost has, of course, in no way altered the marginal cost curve of the second firm. Hence, the price and output policy of the cab monopoly is not affected by the transfer of the franchise. It still produces *OA* units and sells at a price *OD*.

Consider next the case of a Kansas farmer who, in the 1880s, preempts from the public domain an exceptionally fertile piece of wheat land. He farms profitably for his purely competitive market by equating price to marginal cost. As figure 4.3 indicates, he sells *OA* units at a price *OD* and gains a profit (or fertility rent) *EBCD*. Now let the Kansas farmer lease

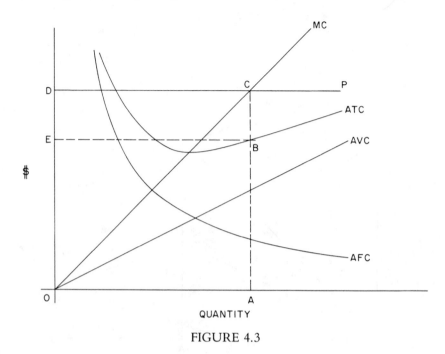

FIGURE 4.3

the land to a tenant. He will charge a rental equal to his profit *EBCD*. This rental becomes an additional element in the fixed cost of the tenant; so that the tenant regards himself as facing the costs depicted in figure 4.4. Again we note that the capitalization process both raises and changes the shape of the curve of average total cost. The first firm produces *OA* units where average total cost was rising. The second firm, which must pay a rental *EBCD* for the land, appears to produce *OA* units where average total cost is at a minimum.

This simple demonstration of how monopoly profit and rent are capitalized into "average cost" by ownership transfers serves, I believe, to drive home three truths often neglected in economics. First, in all firms at all times average cost 'tends' toward average revenue irrespective of the degree of competition prevailing in the factor or product markets.[1] When factors are free to move, and none can command a rent, the equality is produced by factor movements and the concomitant changes in output.

[1] For another formulation of this truth, see the remarks of Milton Friedman on average cost in *Business Concentration and Price Policy*, National Bureau of Economic Research (1955), pp. 230–38.

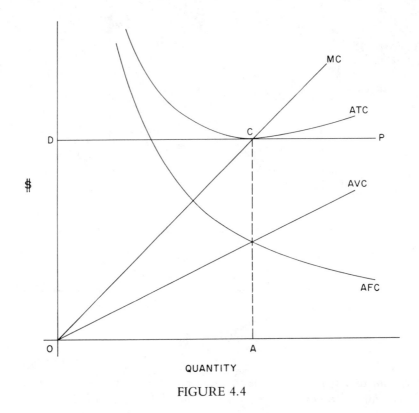

QUANTITY

FIGURE 4.4

When these conditions are not present, the equality is produced by the capitalization of the surplus (rent, or monopoly profit) into factor costs.

Unfortunately, the distinction between rent as a surplus and cost as a necessary factor payment has become a fruitful source of confusion. The distinction supposes that the cost of a factor should be reckoned at what the factor could command in some other use. In the case of a "permit to operate taxicabs," no problem arises since in a purely competitive market the value of such a license (which is only a piece of paper) would be null in any other use.

In the case of wheat land, one is driven back to some venerable issues of methodology. The size of the rent element in the tenant's payment to the landlord depends on the perspective chosen; and there are as many possible rents as there are possible perspectives.[2] From the tenant's standpoint, there is no surplus payment; if he did not pay the owner's price,

---

[2]For another statement of the view that rent is a matter of perspective, see A. P. Lerner, *The Economics of Control* (1944), pp. 218–20.

he would not get the land. From Henry George's standpoint, the whole of the payment to the landlord is rent since, if all payments for the use of all land were appropriated by the State, neither the composition nor the aggregate supply of farm output would change. As a third possibility, one can make "rent" equal to the difference between what an acre of land can command in wheat production and what it could command if devoted to the next most profitable crop. Since the supply of wheat land can be increased or decreased by shifting acreage to or from other uses, a curve of total cost (and, hence, average total cost) can be envisaged for a wheat farmer. One derives the total cost of producing wheat on a given piece of ground by deducting from the landlord's income any sum above the payment needed to persuade him to keep the plot in wheat production.

This last method of reckoning average cost is frequently adopted in modern economic analysis, though it is difficult to see why. If we wish to show how the individual firm selects the price-output policy that maximizes profit in the short run (i.e., when plant and equipment are fixed), it does not matter whether average total cost is defined to include or exclude factor rent or, indeed, whether average total cost is defined at all. Only marginal cost can influence the price-output decision in the short run. If we wish to show how the investment decisions of the individual firm are guided by the profitability of its operations we must, of course, define average cost to include rent. If our object is to make the point that how one defines a factor rent depends upon the perspective chosen, there is no merit in concentrating upon a single perspective, i.e., the industry. Much confusion could be avoided if authors who discuss cost and rent would specify whether their viewpoint is the firm, the industry, the domestic economy, or the world economy.

One cannot say that average total cost should—or should not—be defined to include a rent element, since different tasks require different tools. But let us recognize that these two cost functions may have little in common except the name.

A second neglected truth is implicit in the foregoing remarks. As expounded in all economics textbooks—and most treatises, as well—the notion of average cost of production is useful for one purpose only. It conveys some idea of how the individual firm judges the profitability of its operations. It provides no basis for estimating the social efficiency of the firms in question. One shudders to think how many textbooks in the last thirty years have confidently asserted, with the aid of diagrams taken from Robinson and Chamberlin, that "imperfect competition leads to an equilibrium in which firms are of less than optimum size."

Finally, an awareness of the limitations of the average cost notion should end once and for all the misguided efforts of economists and statisticians to construct average cost functions from empirical data. (Management consultants may legitimately continue in this activity, since their clients are only interested in the average cost functions that enter into the computation of profit. These functions perforce include rents capitalized into factor costs and can be fashioned from empirical data.)

To date virtually all studies of average cost in the business world have reached the same conclusion, i.e., that most firms most of the time operate at an output where average total cost is falling.[3] The only significant inferences to be drawn from these studies are (1) competition in most industries is imperfect—which we knew already, and (2) factor markets do an excellent job of rapidly capitalizing rents and monopoly profits into factor costs—which we ought to have suspected. Apparently, the capitalization process is so much taken for granted in this world that its significance for the interpretation of textbook cost curves and empirical cost data is commonly overlooked.

---

[3]For representative studies reaching this conclusion, see W. J. Eiteman and G. E. Guthrie, "The Shape of the Average Cost Curve," 42 *Am. Econ. Rev.* 832 (1952), and Joel Dean, *Statistical Determination of Costs with Special Reference to Marginal Costs* (1936). For surveys of empirical work on cost functions, see P. J. D. Wiles, *Price, Cost, and Output* (1956), and J. Johnston, *Statistical Cost Analysis* (1960).

5.

Industrial Concentration and the Rate of Profit: Some Neglected Theory

I T IS WIDELY believed that the number of sellers in a market has something to do with monopoly and, indeed, that "degree of concentration" is a measure, or at least an index, of monopoly power. The popularity of this conviction is partly traceable to the way in which basic economics is taught. Sophomores learn that competition is perfect if, and only if, the market contains a large number of sellers of a homogeneous product. Little effort is made to stop beginning students from drawing the tempting but incorrect inference that the fewer the number of sellers, the less competitive the market. The inference is incorrect because there is no meaningful monopoly power unless a firm is collecting a monopoly rent and this power requires an entry barrier. To place the label of "monopoly" on the last remaining firm in a declining industry that no one wishes to enter is a fanciful and highly misleading use of language. Nor is any good purpose served by placing the label on the first firm to enter a new industry.

By themselves, measures of concentration are of little interest to economists (or anybody else, for that matter). However, over the years a great

Reprinted from *The Journal of Law and Economics* (April 1976), vol. 19, no. 1.

Many critics have kindly borne with me in the preparation of this paper. My debts are especially heavy to Richard Brief, David Colander, Ronald Grieson, L. E. Preston, W. G. Shepherd, and William Vickrey.

many studies have indicated that there is a positive association between rates of return on capital in an industry and its degree of concentration. The association has not gone unchallenged by a minority of investigators, mostly from the University of Chicago. After reading through the controversy, my conclusion was that the association between profitability and concentration was real enough but that to attribute it to "monopoly power," as is often done, is no explanation at all. As the first course in statistics teaches, correlation is not causation.

This article was an effort to use basic price theory to determine the association between industrial concentration and rate of return that we can expect to find in industries not closed to new entrants by law. Its outcome was to suggest that in the absence of perfect competition, free entry cannot be expected to equalize rates of return on capital throughout the economy and that this result has a simple explanation. Many markets can provide above average rates of return for n firms but only losses for $n + 1$ firms.

For many years, economists, lawyers, revolutionaries, presidential speech writers, corporate promoters, and—no doubt—other groups as well have been concerned with the possible connections between industrial concentration and profit rates. The persistence of this concern is not surprising. Nor is the acrimonious debate that it has often inspired. After all, if concentration and profitability are not positively correlated, certain fundamental assumptions of classical Marxism, most varieties of nonclassical Marxism, American populism (especially as manifested in antitrust policy) and the modern Schumpeterians are simply wrong. Conversely, if these two variables are positively correlated, libertarian economists and others who place their faith in contactual freedom as a force that will finally erode any above average rate of return must needs rethink their position.

Over the years, many empirical studies have probed for an association between industrial concentration and profitability.[1] But these efforts have

[1]Joe S. Bain, Industrial Organization 452 (2d ed. 1968); Yale Brozen, "The Antitrust Task Force Deconcentration Recommendation," 13 *J. Law & Econ.* 279 (1970); Norman R. Collins and Lee E. Preston, *Concentration and Price-Cost Margins in Manufacturing Industries* (1968); Michael K. Evans, "An Industry Study of Corporate Profits," 36 *Econometrica* 343 (1968); Federal Trade Commission, *Economic Report on the Influence of Market Structure on Profit Performance of Food Manufacturing Companies* (1969); I. N. Fisher and G. R. Hall, "Risk and Corporate Rates of Return," 83 *Q. J. Econ.* 79 (1969); H. Michael Mann, "Seller Concentration, Barriers to Entry, and Rates of Return in Thirty Industries, 1950–1960," 48 *Rev. Econ. & Stat.* 296 (1966); Richard A. Miller, "Marginal Concentration Ratios and Industrial Profit

employed no standardized methodology or set of definitions and, inevitably, have covered different time spans. It is understandable that their results provide no definite answer to the question: What is the correlation between industry concentration and industry rate of return on capital? In this writer's opinion, the most that can be said is that the empirical studies, on balance, seem to show a weak positive correlation.[2]

In any event, as we all used to learn in the under undergraduate statistics course, correlation is not causation. Our intellectual self-respect would seem to require that we consider the answer that can be obtained by applying conventional price theory to the problem. Quite surprisingly, this seems never to have been done. One possible reason for the neglect is that, to date, the tie between industrial concentration and profitability has mainly interested two groups whose first love is not economic theory: statisticians with a professional interest in measurement technique and industrial organization specialists with strong policy biases.

It is true that much effort has gone into calculating the equilibrium prices and outputs implied by the many different models of oligopoly. But to my knowledge, virtually no effort has gone into calculating the equilibrium profit rates implied by those models.

In this paper, we shall try to remedy part of this oversight. To this end, let us begin with the obvious. Industry concentration cannot be causally related to industry profitability in the long run unless it is also causally related to the industry's conditions of entry. So far as causation is concerned, there are three—and only three—possibilities.

1. The industry concentration ratio is affected by the conditions of entry (the limiting case being a public utility monopoly that owes its existence to an exclusive franchise). When causation runs this way, concentration per se cannot constitute a barrier to entry; it is merely the visible evidence that a barrier to entry exists. Nor, when causation runs this way, will trust-busting do anything to promote the entry of new firms (beyond the "artificial insemination" involved in the creation of new firms out of old by government fiat).

Rates: Some Empirical Results of Oligopoly Behavior," 34 *So. Econ. J.* 259 (1967); George J. Stigler, *Capital and Rates of Return in Manufacturing Industries* (1963); Leonard W. Weiss, "The Concentration-Profits Relationship and Antitrust" in *Industrial Concentration: The New Learning* 184 (Columbia Law School Conference on Industrial Concentration. Harvey J. Goldschmid et al., ed. 1974).
[2]For a survey of the evidence that finds a much closer connection between concentration and profitability, see William G. Shepherd, *Market Power and Economic Welfare* (1970), pp. 181–94.

2. The industry concentration ratio itself affects the conditions of entry. The premise that causation runs in this direction plays some part in virtually all theories of so-called predatory competition. Unhappily, while these theories are very numerous, they have not been carefully formulated, so that it is not always clear how concentration is supposed to be a barrier to entry.[3] One view seems to imply that a large firm or a tightly organized cartel is able to wage a more effective price war against a newcomer than a larger number of smaller firms.

3. Some combinations of possibilities 1 and 2, that is, causation, run both ways. Rightly, or wrongly, many economists believe that entry into the production of digital computers in the United States is made difficult both by Nature (in the form of scale economies, great uncertainty, etc.) and by the arsenal of defensive pricing tactics available to the International Business Machines Corporation.

In this paper, we shall be concerned with possibility 1 exclusively. We limit our attention to it for two reasons. First, it is the only one compatible with any variety of static price theory which assumes complete information—known wants, known resources, and a perfect capital market—and the free entry and exit of firms. In contrast, a theory of inter-firm warfare necessarily supposes that rival firms act upon the basis of incomplete information; if it were not so, they would always find it more profitable to cooperate than to engage in price wars.[4]

Second, many otherwise careful writers imply that if entry is free in the textbook sense, rates of return must tend, in the long run, to some uniform level. When this does not happen in the real world, they infer that the industries in question are characterized by barriers to entry that misallocate resources. We shall see that neither the implication nor the inference has a solid foundation in price theory. We shall find that a simple fusion of price theory and probability theory will show that, when competition is imperfect (as it must be in any high concentration industry), free entry will not equalize profit rates among industries even in the long run.

Indeed, we shall find that when the rate of profit is equated with some rate of return on capital, it is possible for any rate of profit to be an equilibrium rate, even though entry into the industry is free. (This superficially

---

[3]For a discussion of the problem of formulating a theory of predatory competition, see L. G. Telser, "Cutthroat Competition and the Long Purse," 9 *J. Law & Econ.* 259 (1966); and B. S. Yamey, "Predatory Price Cutting; Notes and Comments, 15 *J. Law & Econ.* 129 (1972).
[4]This point has been elaborated in Wayne A. Leeman, "The Limitations of Local Price Cutting as a Barrier to Entry," 64 *J. Pol. Econ.* 329 (1956); and Donald Dewey, *The Theory of Imperfect Competition: A Radical Reconstruction* (1969), pp. 104–21.

surprising, not to say staggering, result will turn out to have a very simple explanation.)

To avoid unnecessary semantical complications, it seems advisable to make one feature of our terminology clear at the outset. We shall shortly posit both that entry into the industry is "free" and that every firm has a fixed cost of production and hence decreasing unit cost over some range of output. In a very real sense, the resulting economies of scale do constitute a barrier to entry. But they are not, for this reason, usually regarded as incompatible with what most economists call free entry. The reader is invited to check this judgment against the treatment of the firm in any popular textbook or treatise.

Unfortunately, in the industrial organization literature, a semantical confusion intrudes because economies of scale are almost never discussed, in isolation, as a barrier to entry. They are almost always discussed along with the alleged imperfections of the capital market, investment uncertainty, "unfair" methods of competition allegedly open to big firms, learning costs, etc. In the industrial organization literature, a further confusion intrudes because, among many friends of antitrust who contribute to it, there is a deep-rooted reluctance to believe that economies of scale explain why some firms appear to earn persistently high profits. Surely, they seem to insist, there is more to "market power" than this! Perhaps they are correct. Nevertheless, we shall see that while economies of scale per se may or may not explain persistently high profits in the real world, they do insure that, in any model of oligopoly, the rate of profit can permanently exceed the competitive rate even though entry is free.

In this paper, then, we have two main concerns. (1) When our object is to perceive the connection between profitability and industrial concentration, what measure of profitability should be used? (In the simple oligopoly model that we shall use, measuring industrial concentration is not a problem.) (2) What rates of profit—assuming that profitability has been correctly defined—are consistent with industry equilibrium?

We investigate these issues with two different definitions of profitability. We shall first view the rate of profit as a percentage of sales (revenue) and then as payments to capitalists as a return on capital. These are, of course, the definitions of profitability most commonly employed (though often with modifications) in empirical work on profitability and industrial concentration. Most academic economists (in contrast to many business economists) probably favor the definition which makes the rate of profit a return on capital. We shall presently see that this preference has a weaker theoretical foundation than is generally realized.

We proceed to prove three very general theorems.

A THEOREM ON PROFIT-SALES RATIOS AND INDUSTRIAL CONCENTRATION

Assume:

ASSUMPTION A1. Entry is free in the usual sense of the phrase: The entry of newcomers is not impeded by legislation, ignorance, an imperfect capital market, or technological handicap.

ASSUMPTION A2. The industry consists of firms with identical cost functions which produce a homogeneous product.

ASSUMPTION A3. The total cost curve for each firm is continuous over the economically relevant range of output and "normal" in that total cost never decreases as output increases, that is, marginal cost is always non-negative.

ASSUMPTION A4. All producers are rational and quick-witted oil-gopolists; whatever the aggregate output of the industry, it is always divided equally among the member firms; and "everybody knows" that any price or output change on the part of one producer will immediately be matched by all others. (We here assume what is sometimes called the Chamberlin model of oligopoly.)[5]

ASSUMPTION A5. The industry is in n-firm equilibrium if (1) each of n firms earns a non-negative profit and (2) the entry of an additional firm would make profit negative for all firms.

A comment on these assumptions is offered in section 5 of this paper. The geometry of assumption A4 is given for ready reference in figure 5.1. Here the demand for each is given by ED when the industry consists of 1 firm; by EC for each firm when the industry consists of 2 firms; by EB for each firm when the industry consists of 3 firms; etc. Thus $OC = 1/2 \cdot OD$; $OB = 1/3 \cdot OD$; and $OA = 1/4 \cdot OD$.

We use the following notation:

x = output at which the firm earns its maximum profit in n-firm equilibrium

$s(x) = s$ = total revenue realized by the firm when x is produced

$t(x) = t$ = total cost incurred by the firm when x is produced

$z(x) = z = s - t$ = profit per firm in n-firm equilibrium

---

[5]The computational advantage of the Chamberlin model is considerable: it allows the demand function of the firm to be derived directly from the demand function of the industry. Let demand for the product of an n-firm industry be given by $a - bf(x)$ when $a > b > 0$. Then demand for each firm is simply $a - nbf(x)$.

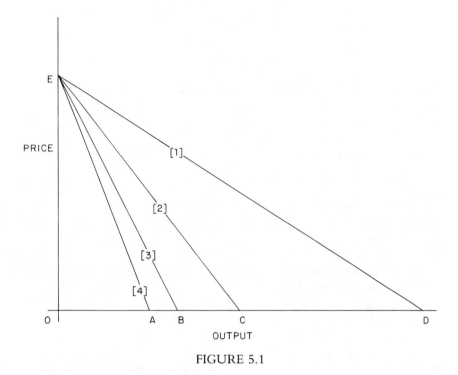

FIGURE 5.1

$r = z/s$ = the profit-sales (revenue) ratio in n-firm equilibrium

sup z = the least upper bound of the set of profits (z's) consistent
with n-firm equilibrium

sup r = the least upper bound of the set of profit-sales ratios (r's)
consistent with n-firm equilibrium

Given the assumptions set down above, it is possible to derive the following theorem.

THEOREM 1. In every industry the profit-sales ratios (r's) consistent
with n-firm equilibrium form the bounded set R on the half-open
interval

$$[0, 1/(n + 1)); \text{ that is,}$$
$$R_n = [r|0 \leq r < 1/(n + 1)] \tag{5.1}$$

This theorem says, inter alia, that if the industry contains n firms in
equilibrium, the profit-sales ratio in each firm must be less than $1/(n + 1)$

but no less than zero.[6] The proof of theorem T1 is not difficult. Since, by assumption A5, profit cannot be negative in n-firm equilibrium, $r \geq 0$.

In a Chamberlin model (with its equal market shares), output per firm is always reduced when an additional firm enters the market. And by assumption A3, marginal cost is always non-negative. Now suppose that $nz \geq t$. Then since the entry of the $(n + 1)$ firm cannot cause t to increase, the $(n + 1)$ firm will enter and claim an equal share of the market, but still leave profit non-negative for all $(n + 1)$ firms. Hence, in n-firm equilibrium we must have $nz < t$ and $z < t/n$. By definition, $z = s - t$ and $r = z/s$; so that we obtain, by substitution, $r < 1/(n + 1)$.

The economic meaning of $1/(n + 1)$ as the least upper bound of the set of profit-sales ratios consistent with n-firm equilibrium is illustrated by figure 5.2. Here EC is the demand curve facing each firm when the industry consists of 2 firms; EB is the demand curve facing each firm when the industry consists of 3 firms. (Lines EC and EB are reproduced from figure 5.1.) Let the unit cost curve for each firm be given by the rectangular hyperbola JJ' which is tangent to EB at point W. Here marginal cost is zero. Should the industry contain 2 firms, each will maximize profit by producing output OQ.

In figure 5.2, $LW = 2/3 \ LV$. Therefore, the rectangle under point W has an area equal to two-thirds the area of the rectangle $OQVL$. Since JJ' is a rectangular hyperbola, the area of the rectangle under point W is equal to the area of the rectangle $OQUM$. Hence, $MUVL$ (total profit) $\div$ $OQVL$ (total revenue) $= 1/3$ or $1/(n + 1)$.

However, given the data in figure 5.2, a 2-firm equilibrium is not really possible if entry is free. Should the industry consist of 2 firms, the profit $UVLM$ will draw a third firm into the industry; the demand curve for each of the 3 firms will be EB; and each of the 3 firms will produce an output at which profit is zero. Thus, when $n = 2$, $1/(n + 1)$ is the upper bound which r may approach but not equal.

Theorem T1 incorporates the "obvious" but neglected truth that an equilibrium under conditions of oligopoly is usually characterized by what is usually (if inaccurately) called monopoly profit. This truth is neglected, we may suspect, mainly because too many textbooks and treatises offer only a perfunctory description of the tangency solution taken from Robinson and Chamberlin. That is, they depict equilibrium under conditions of oligopoly with free entry as one wherein entry has eliminated all profit for all firms.

---

[6]A less austere version of theorem T1 is briefly discussed in Donald Dewey, *Microeconomics: The Analysis of Prices and Markets* (1975), pp. 159–61.

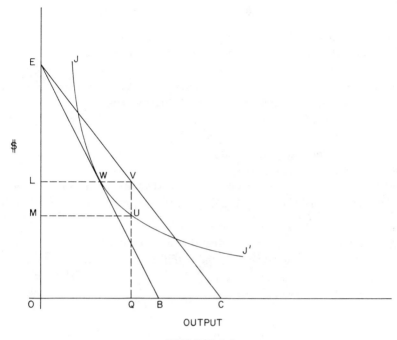

OUTPUT

FIGURE 5.2

It is mathematically possible that the entry of the *n*th firm exactly eliminates all profit for all *n* firms. But on virtually any set of assumptions appropriate to oligopoly, such an outcome is awfully unlikely. It is far more probable that the entry of the *n*th firm will leave profit which is positive but too small to induce the entry for the $(n + 1)$ firm. (This point has been made by several writers over the years, but its implications seem never to have been spelled out for the connection between profit rate and concentration.)[7] Moreover, such residual profits, when they occur in the real world, are often quickly capitalized into the curve of unit cost and so lost to casual view.

Some residual of profit then is likely to be present in any equilibrium under conditions of oligopoly. The exact amount of this residual is governed, of course, by the cost and revenue functions that characterize the industry. And since various combinations of cost and revenue functions are possible, various equilibrium profits (including a zero profit) are possible.

[7]See, for example, George J. Cady, *Entrepreneurial Costs and Price: A Reconsideration of Competitive and Monopolistic Market Theory* (1942), p. 76; or E. H. Phelps Brown, *A Course in Applied Economics* (1951), pp. 32–33.

A THEOREM ON THE DISTRIBUTION OF PROFIT-SALES RATIOS

Figure 5.2 is useful for emphasizing another important truth. In n-firm equilibrium, the profit-sales ratio is likely to lie closer to the lower bound (zero) than to the least upper bound $1/(n + 1)$. In figure 5.2, any unit cost curve that is tangent to the demand curve EC between points E and V (that is, where the absolute value of price elasticity is unity or greater) is compatible with a 2-firm equilibrium. The rectangular hyperbola JJ' is the only unit cost curve (not intersecting EB) that gives $r = 1/(n + 1)$. Thus a necessary but not sufficient condition for $r = 1/(n + 1)$ is that marginal cost be zero for all rates of output.

We can formalize the expectation that, in n-firm equilibrium, a smaller profit-sales ratio is more probable than a greater profit-sales ratio with the following assumption.

ASSUMPTION A6. The probability that any feasible profit-sales ratio $r(0 \leq r < 1/(n + 1))$ will be the equilibrium ratio in n-firm equilibrium is given by $Pr\ r = \alpha - \beta r$ subject to (1) $\alpha - \beta r = 0$ when $r = 1/(1 + n)$ and (2)

$$\int_0^{1/(1+n)} (\alpha - \beta r)dr = 1. \tag{5.2}$$

By assumption A6 we say that the probability that any value for r consistent with n-firm equilibrium will, in fact, be the equilibrium value is a decreasing linear function of r. Thus, the probability distribution of profit-sales ratios consistent with n-firm equilibrium is "right triangular." And as basic statistics books demonstrate, with such a right triangular distribution of probabilities, the expected mean is equal to 0.333 of the range and the expected standard deviation is equal to 0.25 of the range.[8] Writing $\bar{r}$ for the expected mean value of r and σ for the expected standard deviation of r, we can state the following theorem. $(1/(n + 1)$ is, of course, the range of values for r consistent with n-firm equilibrium.)

THEOREM T2. $\bar{r} = 0.333/(n + 1)$ and $\sigma = 0.24/(n + 1)$. (5.3)

How "reasonable" are the relationships between profit-sales ratios and industrial concentration implied by our two theorems? An inspection of table 5.1 indicates that they certainly will not surprise any student of the empirical literature on profitability and market structure.

[8]See, for example, W. Edwards Deming, *Sample Design in Business Research* (1960), p. 260.

TABLE 5.1. Equilibrium Profit-Sales Ratios

Firms n	Mean r	Maximum sup r	Standard Deviation σ
1	0.167	0.500	0.120
2	0.111	0.333	0.080
3	0.083	0.250	0.060
4	0.067	0.200	0.048
5	0.056	0.167	0.040
6	0.048	0.143	0.034
7	0.042	0.125	0.030
8	0.038	0.111	0.027
9	0.033	0.100	0.024
10	0.030	0.091	0.022

Consider the case of 3-firm equilibrium. As table 5.1 shows, when $n = 3$, an equilibrium value for r that approximates an upper bound of 0.25 is possible. But in 3-firm equilibrium the expected mean value of r is only 0.083 with a standard deviation of 0.060. Note that maximum and means values for the equilibrium profit-sales ratio asymptotically approach zero as the equilibrium number of firms increases.

A THEOREM ON CAPITAL RATES OF RETURN

As already noted, while business economists generally keep a sharp eye on profit-sales ratios (if only because sales data tend to be up-to-date and relatively reliable), academic economists, being interested in resource allocation, have usually preferred to express profitability in terms of profit as a return on capital. (Some have preferred to make the denominator total capital; others have argued for equity capital.) Therefore, let us consider how our results would be affected if we redefine profitability to respect this preference. We define the rate of return on capital to be

$$y = (z + ik)/k \qquad (5.4)$$

where z is again total profit (that is, $z = s - t$), i is the rate of interest and k is the quantity of capital. The term $(z + ik)$ denotes "total payments to capitalists" on the assumption that they collect both their "normal" income ik and all of the residual profit z.

We can write $ik = t$, and

$$t = ik + (1 - \lambda)t \qquad (5.5)$$

where t is again total cost and $\lambda(0 \leqslant \lambda \leqslant 1)$ gives the fraction of total cost paid for use of capital. Equation (5.5) merely says that there are two kinds of cost: the normal cost of capital ik and all other costs (wages, etc.) which are $(1 - \lambda)t$.

We can now state and prove our third theorem about profits.

THEOREM T3. For every industry, the rates of return on capital (y's) consistent with n-firm equilibrium form a bounded set whose greatest lower bound is i and whose least upper bound is

$$\sup y = i(1 + \lambda n)/\lambda n. \tag{5.6}$$

Here again it is only the least upper bound (this time sup y) that need concern us. For $y < i$ would contradict assumption A5 which says that profit must be non-negative in n-firm equilibrium. From equation (5.5) we have $k = \lambda t/i$. By theorem T1 we know that in n-firm equilibrium $nz < t$ and sup $z = t/n$. Substituting for k and z in equation (5.4), we have

$$\sup y = i(1 + \lambda n)\lambda n. \tag{5.7}$$

This is a most startling result. It confirms two truths that we already knew: that the rate of return on capital in oligopoly is a function of the rate of interest and the number of firms. But it also shows what is generally overlooked: that the rate of return on capital in oligopoly is also a function of the ratio of capital cost to total cost. Consequently, provided that $y \geqslant i$, any non-negative rate of return on capital is consistent with n-firm equilibrium; and sup $y \to \infty$ as $\lambda \to 0$. In fine, in our simple oligopoly model, the assumption that entry is free places an upper bound on the set of profit-sales ratios (r's) consistent with equilibrium; but this assumption does not place a similar upper bound on the equilibrium rates of return on capital (y's) until positive values of i and λ are specified.[9]

[9]One critic believes that the relationship of λ and n should be clarified because it is not immediately obvious that they are independent variables. As we have seen, n is a function of the ratio of fixed cost to variable cost (since this ratio affects the shape of the curve of average total cost). Many elementary theory textbooks seem to imply that all capital costs are fixed while all noncapital costs are available. This treatment of cost is an inaccurate description of the real world and a simplification of very limited pedagogical usefulness. Fixed costs can be both capital and noncapital.

In our Chamberlin model of oligopoly with free entry, the firm in n-firm equilibrium can only earn the maximum profit-sales ratio consistent with equilibrium when all costs are fixed. (This, to repeat, is a necessary condition, not a sufficient cause.) When all costs are fixed, it is possible that $r \approx 1/(n + 1)$; hence sup r is solely a function of n and is independent of λ. But sup y is a function of both n and λ. For if the value of t is held constant, a change in λ will affect sup y even though it affects neither sup r nor n.

In economics, arresting results usually are either wrong or easily explained. In this instance, a simple and correct explanation is contained in our assumptions that (1) every firm has a fixed cost and (2) production is carried on with two or more factors. So long as the entry of an additional firm will make the industry unprofitable for all firms, that is, force z below zero, no value taken by y will trigger the entry of an additional firm in n-firm equilibrium.

Do our results invalidate the methodology of the many empirical studies which have sought to relate the return on capital to industrial concentration? Probably not. But what may save this methodology is the fact that, in the real world, the values for λ almost always fall within the rather narrow range of 0.10 to 0.30. Hence, in cross-sectional analysis, it is reasonable to expect that the rate of return on capital will vary directly with the industry concentration ratio in high-concentration industries.

Once again, we note that our model yields results which will not surprise any empirical investigator. Suppose that we assign the eminently plausible values $n = 4$, $\lambda = 0.25$, and $i = 0.08$. Then $0.08 \leq y < 0.16$. Moreover, for reasons already developed, any reasonable assumption about the distribution of the profits consistent with n-firm equilibrium will, in this example, place the expected value of y closer to 0.08 than to 0.16.

A Word on Assumptions

THE MAIN implications of our analysis for public policy are two: (1) Free entry can, but probably will not, eliminate the profit residual in an oligopoly market in the long run. (2) The maximum profit-sales ratio consistent with n-firm equilibrium asymptotically approaches zero as n increases.

Would these implications be falsified if our assumptions were modified in the interest of greater realism? I think not. Assumptions A1, A2, and A3, and A5 are employed in virtually all types of partial equilibrium analysis and need not be defended here.

Assumption A4, specifying the Chamberlin model of oligopoly, made all producers rational and quick-witted oligopolists whose behavior insures that aggregate output will, at all times, be divided equally among themselves. This model was employed first, because, with its obvious limitations, it is as realistic as any discernible alternative (probably more realistic where firms are few); and secondly, because it simplifies the algebra.

Our technique for identifying the least upper bounds of the sets of profit-sales ratios and rates of return on capital consistent with n-firm equilibrium can be applied to any free-entry model of oligopoly. Choice of oligopoly model affects these upper bounds but not, we may conjecture, by very much. Choice of model will, of course, have even less effect on median and mean values.

Assumption A6 is unrealistic in one respect only; it makes the probability that any feasible rate of profit will, in fact, be the equilibrium rate a decreasing linear function of its size. I plead that, here, any loss of realism inflicted by the property of linearity is out-weighted by the immense improvement in exposition that it makes possible. In any event, assumption A6 plays no part in the proof of theorems T1 or T3. The least upper bound of the set of profit rates consistent with the stability of n-firm equilibrium is independent of the probability distribution assumed for these rates.

Summary

IT HAS long been known (though not always remembered) that when competition is imperfect, free entry can lead to an equilibrium wherein each firm earns a residual profit (rent). The lumpiness of investment, imposing as it does a fixed cost upon the firm, can produce this result. In this paper, we have worked with two measures of profitability, the profit-sales ratio and the rate of return on capital. We have seen that the maximum profit-sales ratio consistent with equilibrium is solely a function of the equilibrium number of firms; and that the rate of return on capital consistent with equilibrium is a function of the equilibrium number of firms, the rate of interest, and the fraction of total cost which is capital cost. Our results raise the possibility that empirical workers, in seeking to relate profitability to concentration, may have erred in neglecting the profit-sales ratio in favor of estimating rates of return on capital.

This is not to claim that we have "explained" the apparent positive association between industrial concentration and profitability. For, at the outset, we accepted that industrial concentration per se could conceivably serve to raise barriers to entry and, hence, to increase profits. This would happen if concentration produced an industry that was better able to crush new competition and discourage potential competition (presumably by improving the speed and intelligence of entrepreneurial response to entry threats.)

Standing alone, a persistently high rate of profit (however defined) for a high concentration industry merely indicates that "something" is discouraging the inflow of resources. But such profitability tells us nothing about the nature of this something; it could be public policy, fear of "predatory" competition, recognition that the industry would not profitably support another firm, scarcity of raw materials, an imperfect capital market, and no doubt many others things as well. To ascribe, as so often is done, a high rate of profit in a high concentration industry to its "monopoly power" or "market power" is to evade the investigation of an empirical question by failing to recognize that it exists.

We are now hopefully in a better position to appraise our considerable legacy of empirical work on industrial concentration and profit rates. On the one hand, we are entitled to treat with extreme skepticism the small minority view which holds that there is no apparent connection between profitability and concentration. Regardless of the conditions of entry, a positive correlation between concentration and profitability is to be expected when firms are few. If entry is not free into the industry, the impediment to entry will itself probably account for the exceptional profitability. If entry is free in the usual textbook sense, the analysis of this paper applies. On the other hand, for the reasons noted above, exceptional profitability is not to be taken as conclusive evidence of "monopoly" or "market power." A persistently high rate of profit is not even economically interesting unless it is higher than a reasonable oligopoly model incorporating free entry would lead us to expect.

6.

Information, Entry, and Welfare:
The Case for Collusion

O F THE PIECES in this book, this one had the longest gestation period and drew the sharpest criticism when finally sent into the world. When it was finished, my faith in the possibility of using price theory and welfare economics to make a case for antitrust, except as some sort of second-best policy, was totally gone.

Over the years, I became increasingly uncomfortable with my classroom remarks on cartels. After leaving graduate school, my education in antitrust soon progressed to the point where I correctly taught that "only entry conditions matter"; and that, absent entry barriers, monopoly rents will not persist long enough to be worth worrying about. (Much later, having been exposed to contestable market theory, I revised this injunction to say that only entry and exit conditions matter, but that entry conditions matter most.) What, then, was the justification for the antitrust rule, almost universally approved by American economists, that cartel agreements are illegal per se?

From my student days, I knew that in many, if not most, of the famous antitrust cases involving cartels, entry barriers were negligible; and that

In the preparation of this article, I have imposed on the good nature of many critics. My debts are especially heavy to Joseph Seneca, W. G. Shepherd, and William Vickrey.

the view that there was nothing good to be said for cartels was, at least until recently, a peculiarly American conviction. In other cultures, e.g., Japan and prewar Europe, where there was no comparable popular hostility to cartels, economists were prepared to treat the cartel as a form of business organization that probably had its merits and, at any rate, deserved their serious attention. Therefore, my support for the per se rule against price fixing was always limited to the conjecture that, given its administrative convenience, it was not unreasonable to assume that the rule did more good than harm. In the 1970s, the work of Peter Asch and Joseph Seneca persuaded me that even this defense of the per se rule was invalid. For they found that most large manufacturing firms prosecuted for price-fixing actually earned an average rate of return below that of a matched set of firms that had never run afoul of the Sherman Act. It seemed reasonable to conclude that a study of small firms prosecuted for price-fixing would reveal an even lower rate of return.

As yet, even the harshest critics of antitrust (Dominick Armentano always excepted) continue to support the rule that price-fixing agreements are illegal per se. But the worm of doubt is at work. George Bittlingmayer has demonstrated that the arrangement that figured in the most famous of all American cartel cases, *Addyston Pipe,* was very likely welfare-increasing. Economists should not have been surprised by Bittlingmayer's result. It was never a secret that the major participants in this cartel, following its demise, promptly merged to form the United Pipe & Foundry Company that, under one name or another, has survived for ninety years.

In the last thirty years, many of the propositions about the "monopoly problem" which are used to justify an antitrust policy have been called into question and, in many instances, conclusively disproved.[1] As the intellectual foundations of antitrust have crumbled and collapsed, one has so far retained both its nearly universal acceptance and its academic respectability. Almost without exception, economists and lawyers have continued to assume that the case against price fixing—collusion—is so self-evident that it does not require detailed examination. Indeed, the hostility to price fixing is the one feature of American antitrust that seems to be exportable—witness, for example, its continuing incorporation into the cartel policy of the European Common Market. The purpose of this article is to suggest that even the "evil" of collusion can no longer be taken for granted— and, by implication, that a complete and skeptical review of the conspiracy and tacit conspiracy doctrines of antitrust is called for.

---

[1]See, for example, Robert H. Bork, *The Antitrust Paradox: A Policy at War with Itself* (1978); Harvey J. Goldschmid et al., *Industrial Concentration: The New Learning* (1974); and Richard A. Posner, *Antitrust Law: An Economic Perspective* (1976).

One might claim a certain urgency for this task. In recent years, both the Congress and the antitrust agencies have given a very high priority in antitrust enforcement to increasing the number of prosecutions for price-fixing and information sharing. If we are going down the wrong road, we are traveling at an increasing rate.

In retrospect, it is quite surprising that economists have allowed the case against collusion to go unexamined for so long. After all, the textbook treatment of collusion has always been tautological. It assumes that the object of price-fixing is to increase the rate of return on capital; and that, if entry into the industry is free, price-fixing cannot achieve this goal "in the long run." Therefore, so the textbooks imply, if a cartel endures over time, entry is not free and price-fixing must have achieved its goal of creating a monopoly rent.

One can, of course, argue that price-fixing may be forever attempted—and forever frustrated—when entry into the industry is free, because businessmen are so stupid that they do not learn from experience. Such an assumption is, for good reason, usually rejected by economists. In any event, if it could be substantiated, a legal rule against price-fixing would have to be defended on the strange ground that it protected the public against the folly of businessmen in squandering resources on a vain quest.

The textbook treatment of collusion presumes the existence of barriers to entry and the possibility of monopoly rent. But causal observation shows that in the absence of antitrust harassments, price-fixing will be found, most of the time, in industries where—by any reasonable use of language—entry is free and no obvious monopoly rents are being collected. Every industry that merits the name has at least one trade association. Inside every competently run trade association is a cartel yearning to breathe free of legal restraints.

Nor do we have to rely on casual observation for evidence that collusion will persist even when it does not lead to exceptional profitability. In recent studies,[2] Peter Asch and Joseph Seneca found that industries whose member firms have been prosecuted for fixing by the antitrust agencies actually earned a below-average rate of return on capital.

It is the thesis of this article that the paradox of persisting efforts at price-fixing in industries where entry is free and the rate of return on capital "low" has a plausible explanation; and, indeed, that the explanation has often been advanced by businessmen in their own inarticulate and self-serving way. When businessmen seek to justify price-fixing, they invari-

---

[2]P. A. Asch and J. J. Seneca, "Characteristics of Collusive Firms," 23 *J. Ind. Econ.* 223 (1975) and "Is Collusion Profitable?" 68 *Rev. Econ. Stat.* 1 (1976).

ably do so in terms of "preventing ruinous competition," "achieving a healthy climate for investment," "promoting stable market conditions," or some such reassuring rhetoric. Impatient economists usually translate the businessman's inept defense of price-fixing as a simple desire to maximize profits.[3]

Let us try a different translation. Let us assume that what the businessman is trying to maximize is a utility function with two elements: the expected rate of return on capital and the variance associated with this rate.[4] (I introduce variance into the businessman's utility function simply because it is the most widely used measure of uncertainty; any other statistical measure of uncertainty would serve the purpose of this paper just as well.) In a world of uncertainty, this assumption is obviously more realistic than a premise of simple profit maximization. More important, we shall find that it is more useful for understanding the causes and consequences of collusion.

Given free entry, collusion cannot create a permanent monopoly rent. So much is certain. But it is not immediately apparent how collusion will affect the tradeoff between the rate of return on capital (henceforth called "expected profit") and profit variance. For example, for a given utility level, if collusion reduces profit variance it must, of course, reduce expected profit. Nor is it immediately apparent how collusion affects industry output in a free entry situation.

Given its popular connotations of evil purpose, secret maneuvering, and general wrongdoing, the term collusion is not well suited to the vocabulary of technical economics. What this paper means by collusion is better conveyed by the pedestrian phrase, "cooperative action that affects prices." However, I will continue to speak of collusion because of the term's popularity and brevity. By my usage, the term covers both agreements which directly affect price and output and what the British call information agreements, for example, agreements to share price and production data.

---

[3] In all fairness, it should be mentioned that economists who have studied particular industries (especially so-called distressed industries) have sometimes given a sympathetic hearing to the businessman's defense of collusion. See, for example, the treatment of shipping cartels by Daniel Marx; *International Shipping Cartels: A Study of Industrial Self-Regulation by Shipping Conferences* (1953); see also, George B. Richardson, "The Theory of Restrictive Trade Practices," 17 *Oxford Econ. Papers* 39 (1965).

[4] Suppose that in period t the rates of return on capital, $r_1, r_2, \ldots r_p$ are earned by p firms and that r^* designates the mean rate of return. To simplify the exposition, we shall assume that in period $t + 1$, expected profit is r and profit variance v is $\Sigma(r^* - r_i)^2/p$.

Conventional Assumptions

ASSUMPTION A1. Production takes place through successive periods in an industry where uncertainty cannot be reduced below some minimum which is constant; that is, uncertainty can never be completely eliminated through "learning by doing" even though firms are allowed to exchange price and output data and negotiate agreements governing price and output.

ASSUMPTION A2. The industry consists of firms which sell a homogeneous product, not in a perfect market, but in one made imperfect by the costs of acquiring information—a Marshallian market, for short. (I implicitly use the definition taken from formal information theory which makes information "that which reduces uncertainty.")

ASSUMPTION A3. Entry is free in the usual sense of the phrase: The entry of newcomers is not impeded by legislation, ignorance, an imperfect capital market, or technical handicap.[5]

ASSUMPTION A4. All firms are risk averse and seek to maximize the utility function $U(r,v)$ where r is expected profit and v is profit variance. Thus if $r_1 = r_2$ and $v_1 < v_2$, then $R(r_1,v_1) > U(r_2,v_2)$ while if $v_1 = v_2$ and $r_1 < r_2$, then $U(r_1,v_1) < U(r_2,v_2)$.

ASSUMPTION A5. All firms are replicates of one another; any proposition about one firm is a proposition about every other firm.[6]

ASSUMPTION A6. Let k denote the combination of r and v, and $E(K)$, the set of k's consistent with a size population of firms that is con-

---

[5]Free entry, however, is compatible with the existence of a fixed cost in the firm even though the magnitude of this cost is one of the determinants of the equilibrium number of firms. See chapter 5.

[6]G. Warren Nutter and John H. Moore have argued that competitive behavior—which they equate with a firm's willingness to make unilateral price cuts (their analysis does not cover unilateral price rises)—depends upon differences in the taste for risk among sellers. Such differences clearly place a constraint upon the amount of collusion that will be attempted in a market; in this sense, they promote competitive behavior. But they are not a necessary condition for it. So long as collusion is not costless—and it seldom is—firms will invest in collusion up to the level where its expected marginal benefit equals its expected marginal cost. Under conditions of enduring uncertainty, rival firms, whatever their respective tastes for risk, must expect to make a number of price changes each period. It will ordinarily pay them to coordinate some—but not all—of these adjustments. Hence, there is no good reason to forego the simplification in exposition that assumption A5 makes possible. (All firms have the same taste for risk.) See G. W. Nutter and J. H. Moore, "A Theory of Competition," 19 *J. Law Econ* 39 (1977).

stant over time. Then our industry is in long-run equilibrium if, and only if, $k \in E(K)$. Every k included in $E(K)$ must, of course, have the same utility rank. In this (Marshallian) equilibrium, ex post, different firms will earn different profits and some firms may exit and be replaced by an equal number of others.

Additional Assumptions

THE ASSUMPTIONS set down so far would seem to require no elaboration. They have been so often explicitly employed and defended by economists that their usefulness can be presumed. The remaining assumptions deserve some words of explanation. For while they may well be as widely used as the above assumptions (especially in theorizing about "workable" competition or, more recently, in theorizing about the search process in markets), they are seldom formally stated.

The first of the remaining assumptions is made necessary by the tenacious hold of static price theory on all of us. In the usual textbook model, with its perfect market, the power of the firm to affect price is equated with "monopoly power." In this model, with its Marshallian market, the power of the firm to affect price is traceable to the presence of information costs in the market. This power is a short-run phenomenon in the sense that it would disappear if learning by doing could ever reduce search cost to zero. By assumption A1 this cannot happen. Uncertainty—or entropy to use the term borrowed by formal information theory from statistical mechanics—will not fall below some minimum. Hence, at any moment, the firm in a Marshallian market always possesses the limited power over price that exists because information about prices is not free.[7]

Here we meet a predictable difficulty. When sellers are few in a Marshallian market, the firm may have both types of power—and disentangling their effects is not easy. One complication could be especially troublesome—the well-known result that, when entry is free and forms are few, each firm may produce an output at which unit cost is falling.

In this paper, our concern is with the limited power over price traceable to an imperfect market—not with the power over price traceable to imperfect competition in a perfect market. Therefore, let us get rid of the complications of monopoly power by making the equilibrium number of firms great enough to insure that the single firm believes that, whatever its short-run power to influence price, its unilateral actions cannot affect the average of prices prevailing in the production period. (Just as the used

[7]On the search process in what I have called a Marshallian market, see George J. Stigler, *The Organization of Industry* (1968) pp. 39–66, and Nutter and Moore, "A Theory of Competition."

car dealer can take pride in his skill in bargaining in particular transactions and still believe that it has no perceptible effect on the average of used car prices in his market for the year.) We eliminate the effect of monopoly power due to fewness of sellers by assuming:

ASSUMPTION A7. Let x^* be the output at which unit cost is minimized in the firm. Then whatever the legal rules regarding collusion, in equilibrium the firm's output is expected to fluctuate during the production period about a mean of x^*. (This assumption does not exclude the possibility that the unit cost of x^* is affected by the legal rules regarding collusion.)

The next assumption requires an even more extended introduction. In the perfect market ruled by the Law of One Price, there can be no such thing as price competition. This gives us one more reason for distrusting generalizations about the effects of collusion based upon economic models which assume a perfect market. In our Marshallian market made imperfect by the costs of acquiring information, price competition does exist. It has two features especially relevant to this analysis.

The price changes which firms make during the production period are imperfectly coordinated. Each firm associates more than one possible payoff with every unilateral price change and, for each firm, the pricing behavior of rivals is a source of uncertainty. In general, the greater the number of price changes that they make, the greater this uncertainty.

In a Marshallian market, price changes by the firm serve two related but distinguishable purposes. They are the economic application of information already received. And they are a means of acquiring additional information since, in an uncertain world, some part of the activity of the firm must always involve an exploratory search for information.

Strictly speaking, there can never be price stability in the sense of unchanging prices in a Marshallian market. Firms will, in every period, vary prices to obtain information and the value of any bit of information, once obtained, will decline with the passing of time.[8]

In this analysis, we shall pass to the limit in simplification and use as our index of price competition the total number of price changes made by all firms in the industry during the production period. N will denote this number. Price competition has, of course, more dimensions than the total number of price changes per period; it includes, at the very least, the presence or absence of a discernable pattern of price leadership in the price

[8]Not many efforts have been made to apply formal information theory to economic problems. See, however, Henri Theil, *Economics and Information* (1967) and R. A. Jenner, "An Information Model of Pure Competition," 76 *Econ. J.* 786 (1966).

changes. But little will be lost by equating price competition with the size of N. It is virtually impossible to conceive of any change in price competition that does not involve a change in N. Looking to future empirical work, another merit may be claimed for N as an index of price competition. It can be directly estimated from price data.

Also, the use of the total number of price changes per period as an index of price competition obviates the need for any recondite speculation about how price competition is to be distinguished from collusion. By the usage of this paper, collusion is simply the absence of price competition. In this model, with its Marshallian market, anything that increases N increases price competition and simultaneously reduces collusion, and vice versa.

Nor do we need to get bogged down in efforts to classify the varieties of collusion. It is collusion when firms directly reduce N by agreeing to charge a common price and alter it only when acting together. It is collusion when firms pool their data on prices and costs in order to gain a more accurate picture of "underlying business conditions" and the result is a reduction in N. Collusion may be overt—as in the formal cartel agreement—or implicit—as in the mental telepathy that produces price leadership in highly concentrated industries.

I now state the final three assumptions.

ASSUMPTION A8. Let the legal system be given. Then for every industry output (hereafter designated X) there is a number of price changes which will maximize $U(k)$ for that output. If this number is exceeded, (1) r will fall, (2) v will rise, or (3) r will fall and v will rise.

ASSUMPTION A9. Let the legal system be given. Then the number of price changes which maximizes $U(k)$ for each output varies directly with output.

ASSUMPTION A10. The legal system matters. A rule change which reduces the cost of collusion will, by encouraging agreements to reduce N, have some effect upon r, v, and X.

Let us pause to emphasize one implication of the last three assumptions. Suppose that within a legal system that prohibits collusion, $U(k)$ for an industry could be raised if this prohibition could be ignored with impunity. Suppose also that such is not the case—that the legal system has sufficient teeth (in terms of the severity and probability of punishment) to deter collusion, that is, joint action to reduce N. Then, by our usage, the N that actually results is "optimal." In short, to the extent that legal rules constrain business behavior, the N that is optimal from the industry's standpoint is partly a function of the legal system.

Alternative Legal Systems

WE CAN now consider how the operation of our industry is affected by the law's treatment of collusion. Let us examine three possible legal systems.

1. Alpha System: The industry, in common with all other industries, is subject to a legal code which prohibits, and effectively prevents, collusion. Defendants are ferreted out by an army of informers, tried by courts-martial, enjoy only the due process accorded to privates in the armies of Old Prussia, and, if convicted, sentenced to a reopened Alcatraz.

2. Beta System: The industry is given a total exemption from the above Draconian version of antitrust, while all other industries remain subject to it. To avoid ambiguity, let us make the price and information agreements of the exempted industry legally enforceable though, so far as economic effects go, it probably makes little difference whether the exempted industry uses the courts or private cartel machinery to enforce such agreements.

3. Omega System: There is no antitrust for anyone. In all industries, firms have complete freedom to exchange information and negotiate price agreements. Otherwise assumptions A1–A10 remain in force.

By assumption A10, "the legal system matters." But let us be more specific. (1) How will the granting of an antitrust exemption to a single industry (shifting from the Alpha System to the Beta System) affect its equilibrium output? (2) How will the granting of this exemption affect the equilibrium values of r and v? We know, of course, that $U(k)$—the utility rank of the (r,v) combination—will be the same in both equilibria, since all equilibrium k's must, by definition, have the same rank.

Let us begin by noting an "obvious" truth of crucial importance. For our chosen industry, the set of production possibilities represented by the Beta System of laws completely dominates that of the Alpha System. Any contract that can be negotiated under the Alpha System can also be negotiated under the Beta System, but the converse is not true. Under both legal systems the industry can refrain from colluding. Only under the Beta System is collusion feasible. The implications of this domination are indicated by figure 6.1.

Here the curve $BDEF$ gives the maximum utility rank of the k corresponding to each industry output when produced under the Beta System (our industry alone exempt from antitrust). The curve $ACEF$ gives the maximum utility rank of the k corresponding to each industry output when produced under the Alpha System (antitrust for everyone).

Each curve in figure 6.1 is drawn on the assumption that N has been optimized for each X under the legal system that the curve represents. In accordance with assumption A9, movement along either curve rightward

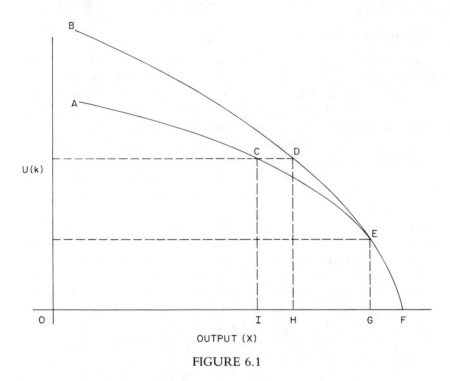

FIGURE 6.1

from the origin implies an increase in N. Likewise, in accordance with assumption A10, whenever the two curves do not coincide, any given X implies a lower N if produced under the Beta System than if produced under the Alpha System. When the two curves coincide in figure 6.1, a given X will be associated with the same N under both systems; this is the case where law does not matter.

Suppose that the utility rank of every k consistent with equilibrium output is given by the vertical distance EG. Then equilibrium output is given by the horizontal distance OG; and OG will be the industry's equilibrium output whether it is produced under the Alpha or Beta System. I have constructed figure 6.1 to incorporate the popular—and perfectly reasonable view—that when the number of firms is "very large," it will not pay an industry to attempt collusion even when it is lawful (by assumption A7, in the model, the number of firms varies directly with industry output). With very large numbers, the contract costs of collusion are simply "too high."

Suppose, however, that the utility rank of every k consistent with industry equilibrium is given by the vertical distance HD (or IC). Now equilibrium output is *OI* under the Alpha System but the greater quantity *OH* under the Beta System.

We have answered our first question. Legalizing collusion in a single industry, when entry is free, will either leave equilibrium output unchanged or cause it to increase. Legalizing collusion will cause equilibrium output to increase when it operates to increase the number of contracts that it is economically rational to negotiate. This conclusion is, of course, perfectly compatible with the possibility—indeed, the virtual certainty—that the immediate short-run consequence of legalizing collusion will be a contraction of industry output to the extent entry is slow to gain a higher *r* and lower *v*. Presumably movement to a new equilibrium will take time.

What of our second question—the effect of legalizing collusion on profit and profit variance? Here figure 6.1 yields an ambiguous and intriguing result. Each of the following outcomes is possible in the new equilibrium: (1) *r* and *v* are unchanged, (2) *r* and *v* are both greater, and (3) *r* and *v* are both lower. The only requirement is that, in the new equilibrium, the combination (*r*,*v*) has the same utility rank as that consistent with equilibrium in the Alpha System.

Why the ambiguity? Surely our initial expectation is that, if collusion is a way of reducing uncertainty, legalizing collusion in an industry where entry is free ought to produce a new equilibrium characterized by lower *r* and lower *v*. The pitfall in this expectation becomes apparent when we recall that the number of price changes per period is a function of both the legal system and the industry's output; and that legalizing collusion can lead to greater output.

Suppose the legalizing collusion does lead to greater output. Then such a change in the law has reduced the optimal *N* associated with each *X* over some range. (This range is given by the distance *OG* in figure 6.1.) However, as the industry moves to a new equilibrium, the increase in *X* produces an increase in *N*. Depending upon the strength of the new opposing forces operating on *N* in the new equilibrium, legalizing collusion will leave *r* and *v* unchanged, lower both *r* and *v*, or raise both *r* and *v*. I can only say the obvious: the greater the increase in output that occurs when an industry is permitted to collude, the more likely that collusion will actually result in higher equilibrium values for both *r* and *v*.

To anyone with a traditional training in economics the conclusion that collusion can increase output is unfamiliar and possibly suspect. Nevertheless, to avoid it one would have to show that the statement that "collusion is effective" is a logical contradiction of one or more of the assumptions that we have employed. So long as collusion confers no benefits on established firms that are not available to new firms, no such demonstration can be made. But if information made possible by collusion is available only to established firms, assumption A3 is contradicted; and they gain a cost advantage over potential rivals that would not exist in the absence of collusion.[9] (In this case, collusion may—or may not—be output-increasing, i.e., collusion may be justified on welfare grounds even though it confers a cost advantage on established firms.) Any possibility that established firms may gain a competitive edge through inside information can, of course, be removed by making open membership a requirement for permitting collusion.

When Collusion Is Everywhere Legal

WHEN ONLY one industry receives an exemption from an otherwise universally enforced legal rule against collusion, the exempted industry can expand output mainly by attracting resources from other industries. If a policy condemning collusion is scrapped for all industries, we cannot say how any particular industry would be affected by this change without further information. The only safe generalization is that resources will move from industries where the rewards from the newly legalized collusion are low to those where they are high.

For the economy as a whole, the effects of legalizing collusion are more easily seen. Collusion will reduce uncertainty and, therefore, the cost of investment and marketing mistakes. In a risk-averse world, collusion by reducing uncertainty will presumably also increase the fraction of national income invested.

Collusion and Economic Welfare

SO FAR, we have stayed strictly within the confines of positive economics. The time has come to be more adventurous, and we need have no hesitation in making the following generalization: In a model incorporating the assumptions used in this analysis (most notably the assumption of free entry), economic welfare will be greater under a legal system that permits collusion than under one which effectively suppresses or restricts it. Still, every economic model has its limitations as a guide to policymaking in the real world. Since 1899 in *Addyston Pipe & Steel Co. v.*

---

[9]An apparent instance of the use of information by insiders to attempt to block the entry of a new firm into the market is described in *Paterson Parchment Paper Company v. Story Parchment Co.,* 37 F(2d) 537 (1st Cir. 1930). In this case, the country's three established producers of parchment paper (then used to wrap meat) refused to accept a newcomer into their long-standing cartel and allegedly engaged in a coordinated effort to drive him from the market.

United States,[10] the hostility of federal courts to collusive price-fixing and information exchanges which may reduce price competition has been, with only very minor exceptions, consistent and implacable.[11] It seems reasonable to believe that this hostility to collusion is founded on something more than bad economic theory and/or the convenience of judges and prosecutors.

To say the obvious: to the extent that entry is impeded, the presumption in favor of permitting collusion is weakened. When the number of sellers in the market is fixed and immutable, Cournot's treatment of oligopoly, especially in its Vickrey version, has at least a modest claim to plausibility as a guide to policy.[12] (Its claim is no more than modest, since Cournot's oligopolists are presumed never to discover any way of exchanging information with one another.)

In the case where entry restrictions are man-made (for example, trucking and FM radio stations), laws against collusion are defensible as a second-best policy. (The industry which has the political influence needed to secure entry controls often has enough to gain an exemption from antitrust rules against price-fixing, but this is another story.) Conceivably, the real world is now so riddled with entry barriers created by tax laws, franchise requirements, safety standards, import quotas, zoning regulations, etc., that a presumption in favor of collusion based on a premise of free entry is not strong enough to justify a major change in our present policy.

In this paper, my analysis (by assumption A7) has been restricted to the case where the number of firms is large enough to insure that each will, in equilibrium, have an expected output at which unit cost is minimized. Would the welfare conclusions be different if the equilibrium number of firms were "small"? While the issue remains to be investigated, there is no immediately obvious reason why they should be different. Recall the justification offered earlier for restricting our analysis to the case of many firms. We accepted that the firm can have power over price because it sells

[10]175 U.S. 211 (1899).

[11]Notably *Appalachian Coals, Inc. v. United States,* 228 U.S. 344 (1933) and *Maple Flooring Ass'n. v. United States,* 268 U.S. 563 (1925).

[12]In the original Cournot model of oligopoly, every oligopolist is presumed to know the demand curve for the product of the industry in which he operates. In the Vickrey version, every oligopolist begins production in total ignorance of this demand curve. It was Vickrey's achievement to show that each oligopolist, acting alone, would ultimately collect sales data which, when analyzed, would lead him to behave as would a Cournot oligopolist. Let Q_e denote equilibrium output, Q_c the output that would be produced under purely competitive conditions (an infinitely large number of sellers), and S the number of sellers. In both the original and the Vickrey version of the Cournot model of oligopoly, $Q_e = SQ_c/(S + 1)$. See A. A. Cournot, *Recherches sur les principes mathématiques de la théorie des richesses,* (1836), trans. by Nathaniel T. Bacon as *Researches into the Mathematical Principles of the Theory of Wealth* (1897); and William S. Vickrey, *Microstatics* (1964), pp. 305–08.

in a market made imperfect by information costs and/or because it is an oligopolist; and I wished to isolate the effects of these two different types of power. But the generalization must stand that collusion cannot permanently reduce output unless it creates a barrier to entry that would not otherwise exist. In the absence of this result, even for oligopolists, collusion can only increase output in the long run.

Finally, there is the argument that can be made in favor of retaining the standard railroad gauge, nonmetric systems of measurement, the state senate of Rhode Island, or any other anachronism of long standing; the social welfare cost of correcting it may be too high. In some industries, the short-run welfare loss that would follow a legalization of collusion would certainly be substantial.

For these reasons, it seems best to refrain (at least for the present) from asserting or implying that the analysis of this paper has shown that legalizing collusion will increase economic welfare. Still, there is no reason why my claims for the analysis should be advanced with timidity. The advocates of strong measures against price-fixing and information exchanges should no longer be allowed to treat the welfare case for their position as nearly self-evident. It is not. Indeed, they must now come forward and argue a proposition which is, on its face, implausible: that economic welfare can be increased by legal rules that penalize the creation of information about markets. The fact that competition, as measured by the frequency of price change, can sometimes be increased by making producers more ignorant about markets is true but not to the point.

At the very least, my analysis provides ample justification for condemning any use of scarce antitrust enforcement resources to harass small-fry price-fixers and low-budget trade associations. Let the local laundries collude in peace.

7.

Antitrust According to Robert Bork: Some Reservations

THE FOLLOWING essay conveys what reading and reviewing Robert Bork's *The Antitrust Paradox: A Policy at War with Itself* did for my own thinking about antitrust. Whatever its imperfections, Bork's book by virtue of its zeal, clarity, and economic rigor is deservedly the most widely read work on antitrust that has appeared in the last thirty years. Like Dr. Johnson's prospect of being hanged in the morning, reading *The Antitrust Paradox* wonderfully concentrates the mind. Though it was not his intention, Bork's insistence that price theory should be the sole organon for evaluating antitrust led me to conclude that, by this test, the policy in its totality must be judged as, at best, ineffective and, at worst, counterproductive. But after reaching this conclusion, I still found myself unwilling to share Bork's animus against most of real world antitrust.

So far as I can tell, the roots of this reluctance are some tangled mix of the Burkean, Machiavellian, and populist: Burkean, because I believe that antitrust deserves the presumption of respect that should be accorded to any bit of statecraft that has lasted for a hundred years; Machiavellian,

I would like to thank Susan Rose-Ackerman and Bruce Bassett for their comments on an earlier draft of this paper. It first appeared in volume III(2) of *Contemporary Policy Issues* (Winter 1984–85) under the title "What Price Theory Can—and—Cannot—Do for Antitrust." The new title, I believe, provides a more accurate description of its contents.

because I believe that antitrust may discourage resort to the state-owned monopolies and price controls properly loathed by economists, East and West; and populist, because the distrust of the political influence of large corporations and their leaders which permeated my upbringing and early education has left its mark. I could respect old Ma Bell but never love her or lament her demise.

What follows below is based on a paper presented at a session of the Western Economic Association at Las Vegas in June 1984. The session was devoted to *The Antitrust Paradox,* the other participants being Thomas DiLorenzo, Jack High, and Robert Bork. For readers familiar with his work over the years, it is hardly necessary to mention that Bork found no merit in any of the criticisms.

When *The Antitrust Paradox* first appeared in 1978, my reaction was mostly one of grateful admiration. The economic analysis was first-rate and straight ahead, free of the involved legalistic glosses that had characterized many earlier treatments of the same issues. The exposition was wonderfully lucid. I did, however, have two serious reservations about then Professor Bork on antitrust. Since they have not gone away, I would like to return to them here. The first involves methodology; the second involves political philosophy, perhaps even religion.

In my review of *The Antitrust Paradox,* I presumed to chide the author for a lack of consistency in methodology.[1] By any reasonable reading, the book is a call to scrap most of antitrust law existing at the time of publication. (Some things have changed since January 1981.) My criticism was that if Bork had rigorously adhered to the test that he lays down for evaluating antitrust rules, he would have gone all the way and repudiated antitrust in its entirety.

Bork holds that conventional price theory[2] is the only acceptable tool for evaluating an antitrust rule, and that no rule is justified unless price theory provides a presumption that it will increase output.[3] He then con-

---

[1]Donald Dewey, "Antitrust and Economic Theory," 87 *Yale L.J.* 1516 (1978).

[2]From internal evidence, it appears that Bork means by conventional price theory the kind taught at Chicago thirty years or so ago. Except for the old Chicago hostility to models of oligopoly, it is still a highly serviceable tool for dealing with antitrust issues. Some subsequent developments—most recently the idea of a contestable market—further eroded economists' belief in antitrust. I know of no development that would provide a basis for refuting any of Bork's negative judgments on the policy.

[3]Some economists (certainly William Vickrey) will object that the correct test of an antitrust rule is not how it affects output, as Bork urges. The preferred test would be impact on economic welfare since it is possible that an antitrust rule, by creating enough excess capacity, can both increase output and reduce economic welfare. This objection is valid but, I believe,

cludes that there are only three proper tasks for antitrust; the suppression of price-fixing agreements (cartels), the blocking of mergers that create large market shares,[4] and the prevention of predation narrowly defined. Bork sees predation as mainly arising out of the abuse of legal procedure. If he is correct—and I certainly do not doubt him—predation presents no problem of price theory that need concern us.

My objection was that while Bork had pledged to ground his evaluations in price theory, he drops this test when he brings forward his recommendations on cartels and mergers. Let me state plainly that I have no objection to the price theory test nor to Bork's use of it when he does use it (which is most of the time). Like Bork, my preference is for clean theory over inconclusive data with a rapid rate of obsolescence. I find wholly valid his largely negative comments on the so-called economic arguments that are used to justify antitrust rules. But theory plays no part in his defense of the small remnant of antitrust that he would preserve.

His case for preserving the rule that price-fixing agreements should be treated as illegal per se is based on the assertion that such agreements serve hardly any purpose beyond the restriction of output. I do not believe that this proposition is factually correct. We have vast literature on cartel agreements around the world, and cost-reducing features can be found in many. However, by Bork's guidelines, the proper appeal is not to data but to theory. Surely the clear, unambiguous implication of conventional price theory is that only entry and exit conditions matter—and that of the two, entry conditions matter most. Unless it can be shown that cartels create entry barriers that would not otherwise exist, they are entitled to the same presumption of welfare creation as any other type of private contract. A price-fixing agreement, after all, is only a stop on the continuum of inter-firm cooperation whose limit is total fusion. If, like Bork, one is willing to accept a merger of firms with small market shares, it is illogical, on welfare grounds, to object to weaker forms of cooperation by such firms.

---

not too important. Somewhere in the history of antitrust there is probably one or more decisions that produced this ambiguous result. Since an example does not come readily to mind, I infer that they are few and far between. A possible example is the 1954 consent decree against Eastman Kodak that vastly increased the number of small photo finishers. *United States v. Eastman Kodak Co.,* CCH 1954 Trade Cases, Para. 67, 920.

[4]In *The Antitrust Paradox,* Bork finally comes out against both mergers that give one firm more than 70 percent of the market (with a suspicion of illegality starting at 40 percent) and mergers that leave fewer than three significant rivals. However, these recommendations are made, in Bork's words, "partly as a tactical concession to current oligopoly phobia and partly in recognition of section 7's intended function of tightening the Sherman Act rule" (p. 221). His "true" preference seems to be for a rule that would permit mergers which encompass up to 60 or 70 percent of the market.

For the record, I am recent convert to this benign view of cartels—so strong were the influences of my youth. Our antitrust inconsistency in harassing small-fry cartels, while tolerating the well-understood signaling of big-firm oligopolies, had long bothered me. However, for years when discussing *Addyston Pipe* (1899)[5] and related cartel cases in class, I hedged by suggesting that a strictly economic approach to antitrust called for "the consideration of each case on its merits." This was the coward's way out. To any of my former students who may read this, I offer my apology. There is no possibility that cartel agreements will be decriminalized in the near future. Therefore, it is not necessary here to pass to the limit and consider whether, on welfare grounds, they should be lawful and enforceable in court or merely lawful. Both approaches have had their advocates at other times and places.

I hope that Bork will forgive me for not resisting the following digression. In *The Antitrust Paradox,* the highest praise for judges—indeed about the only praise for judges—is reserved for William Howard Taft's lower court decision in *Addyston Pipe* (1898).[6] The elaborate cartel in this old case was recently examined by George Bittlingmayer in his doctoral dissertation at Chicago.[7] He concluded that, in the absence of cooperation, there could have been no stable equilibrium, given the industry's structure in the late 1890s. According to Bittlingmayer, the cartel was an attempt at rationalization. Following Taft's decision, part of the cartel was replaced by a merger that produced the United Pipe and Foundry Company (which, I believe, still exists under a different name).

Bork's reasons for retaining a vestigial merger policy are not clear to me. He properly doubts that data on profit rates in high-concentration industries should be accepted as evidence of a tie between concentration ratios and "monopoly power." His only concession to a possible connection is a willingness to accept evidence from some antitrust cases that price sometimes drops sharply when a second firm enters the market. But a price-theory test has been promised; data, whether reliable or unreliable, should not figure in his argument.[8]

---

[5]*Addyston Pipe & Steel Co. v. United States,* 175 U.S. 211 (1899).
[6]*United States v. Addyston Pipe & Steel Co.,* 85 F. 271 (6th Cir. 1898).
[7]Some of Bittlingmayer's results have been published: "Decreasing Average Cost and Competition: A New Look at the Addyston Pipe Case," 25 *J. Law Econ.* 201 (1982).
[8]While the concentration ratios of price theory models are totally inconsequential, data on real-world concentration have some modest value in economic research. Arranged in time series, they can throw some light on what is happening to efficient firm size relative to market demand and on the impact of trust-busting measures. But such data are useless as a basis for inferring whether movement is toward or away from some ideal allocation of resources.

Bork believes that high-concentration industries are closer in economic performance to the competitive model than the monopoly model. He does not, so far as I can see, invoke any theory to explain why this should be so.

Here, I suspect that Bork's ambiguity is traceable to the old Chicago School's inability to come to terms with oligopoly defined as the set of all economic models except those of pure competition, discriminating monopoly, or nondiscriminating monopoly. (How Chicago came to ignore Cournot and to view Edward Chamberlin as an agent of the devil, second in rank only to J. M. Keynes, is an intriguing story but too long to present here.) Bork spends several pages attacking the fallacious conclusions reached by some economists who have used oligopoly models. What Bork says about them is true but, again, not relevant. Any bit of scientific apparatus can be misused—as friends of the pure-competition model should know better than most.

When discussing mergers, Bork is up against the most enduring, and possibly most important, problem in price theory. It can be put quite simply. Suppose that in the absence of an entry barrier, a market can support n firms, but not $n + 1$ firms, and that n is a small, finite, number. What will price and output be in this market? Will output be efficiently produced?

How one answers these questions depends, of course, on the kind of model specified, and there are now many models to choose from. Some models, including the one I favor (chapter 8), yield an efficient solution; some do not. But without a model of oligopoly, these questions have no answers. Until they are answered, we cannot take the next step and infer the welfare consequences of alternative merger policies.

An ironic feature of Bork's attack on oligopoly is that it could have helped him to substantiate his correct (largely negative) conclusions about merger policy. When free entry is assumed, any model of oligopoly can be used to demonstrate that a restraint on mergers can only reduce economic welfare. This is true by definition of models that yield an efficient solution to begin with. If the model points to equilibrium with excess capacity, the creation of additional firms will lead to more excess capacity. Whenever there are "wastes of oligopoly," the welfare-increasing prescription is always more concentration, not less.

Bork emphatically believes—and I emphatically agree—that with free entry, firms that are inefficiently large will not go on collecting an economic rent for very long. He is opposed to the use of trust-busting against a firm which has held its market share, however large, for ten years of more. If one takes this position, why block any mergers? Why not a market test? Let the firms merge and see what happens. Price theory provides no presumption that the welfare gain from blocking mergers which cannot hold their market share will exceed the welfare loss from blocking mergers which can.

Let us be clear that my claim is only that it is the kind of price theory esteemed by Bork—and, I trust, by most of us—which provides no support for antitrust.[9] There are other constructions that are often called by the name of theory. The younger members of our profession are wonderfully adept at devising economic games and scenarios. I do not doubt that, by the careful choice of assumptions, one can argue that almost any rule which the courts or the Federal Trade Commission (FTC) can devise will increase output. Recently, two able economists playing this ad hoc game have even given us a theory of predatory innovation.[10]

I wholeheartedly endorse Bork's use of the price-theory test as a guide to the welfare effects of antitrust rules. Yet, when it comes to policy, we part company. Bork believes that the promotion of consumer welfare should be the single goal of antitrust. If I read him correctly, the sooner this goal is accepted by the courts and the FTC, the better.

If I could see antitrust as a major source of inefficiency in the American economy, I might agree. But by my reading, antitrust is just not a very important policy, so far as its welfare impact is concerned. For better or worse, all business practices have substitutes, and most have close substitutes; and businessmen are quite adept at devising ways to minimize the impact of antitrust rules that reduce efficiency. This is not to say that the welfare loss imposed by present policy is negligible, nor to deny that, until January 1981, it was not growing. But would any economist seriously argue that the welfare loss traceable to antitrust is anywhere nearly as great as, say, the loss inflicted by our tax laws or local zoning regulations?

I have no elaborate case to support the conjecture that antitrust is not a very expensive policy.[11] My strongest argument is simply that if the welfare loss of antitrust were substantial, it would be visible to the naked

[9]The above skeptical view of "economic" arguments for antitrust not grounded in conventional price theory is a change from an opinion offered in my 1978 review of *The Antitrust Paradox*. At that time, I suggested that a perfectly respectable case for antitrust could be constructed from arguments that antitrust generated benign externalities. Such activity may be respectable, but I no longer believe in its usefullness. Given that there is no limit to the number of benign externalities that can be ascribed to antitrust, there is no limit to the number of "special" economic cases that can be constructed for it.

[10]J. A. Ordover and R. D. Willig, "An Economic Definition of Predation: Pricing and Product Innovation," 91 *Yale L.J.* 8 (1981).

[11]For evidence on the pork barrel possibilities of antitrust, see R. L. Faith, D. R. Leavens, and R. D. Tollison, "Antitrust Pork Barrel," 25 *J. Law. Econ.* 329 (1982).

eye. This is not the case. Antitrust has created none of the blatant capitalized monopoly rents associated with regulation. (The franchise value of a single New York taxicab is now about $80,000.) I do believe that, in many industries, antitrust has created and preserved firms that are inefficiently small. The basis for this belief is the conviction rooted in both price theory and business history that if the antitrust laws were repealed, the economy rapidly would become more concentrated. If one believes that market competition tends to produce firms of optimum size, such concentration would be cost-reducing. However, in price theory, either it pays to merge or it does not. Hence, relatively trivial cost savings can trigger sizable changes in concentration ratios.

It is the modest welfare impact of antitrust that produces the awful sense of déja vu that sooner or later overtakes those of us who labor in the antitrust vineyard. Since the welfare impact is small and data on scale economies are soon out of date, strongly held opinions change slowly, if at all. We trot out the same arguments and rebuttals year after year.

Can I offer no better reason than the unimportance of the welfare loss imposed by antitrust for declining to march with Bork? I can try.

Admirers of Edmund Burke can cite persuasive reasons for moving only slowly to change any institution or law of long standing—not excluding grand juries, sheriff's posses, township governments, and bicameral state legislatures. While these reasons apply to antitrust, I would prefer to urge a more directly utilitarian argument for caution in changing antitrust.

Antitrust is good or bad in relation to the alternatives. Bork seems to think that the elimination of the many bad antitrust rules would be followed by a void that would enlarge contractual freedom. I cannot share his confidence. The country has turned its back on the antitrust ideal on only one occasion—in 1933. The result was, of course, the industry "self-government" codes enforced by the short-lived and unmourned National Recovery Administration (NRA). Makes you think.

Personally, I have never been much disturbed about the goals imputed to antitrust by the opinions of the late Justice Douglas nor even about the economic consequences of the opinions. (The use of economics by Justice Douglas is another matter.) A more decentralized, less bureaucratized economy is not an ignoble ideal. If the country is prepared to sacrifice some amount of GNP to realize it, so be it. As far as I know, no one has ever claimed limited liability as a basic human right. Power to write the law of corporations is universally conceded to Caesar. Before dismissing Douglas' ideal as merely one more manifestation of the economic ignorance and incompetence that Justice Holmes complained of, I believe that critics of antitrust should make a good faith effort to understand its appeal.

Having benefited from Schumpeter's instruction, economists should know better than most people that any economic system, and certainly capitalism, generates a great many hostilities and anxieties—some specific, some vague. Whatever their origin or justification, economic policy has to deal with them.

Bork holds that, at the start, antitrust was a policy whose overriding purpose was the promotion of consumer welfare, and that this purpose has been subverted by the courts. I do not agree. By my reading, the Sherman Act was a piece of populist legislation passed in response to a mixed bag of fears—fear of the railroads, fear of the banks, fear of the corporate form, fear of cartels, and, above all, fear of the Standard Oil Company.[12] I do not assert that these fears were justified, only that they were real. Given the low quality of so much of the discussion of the "trust problem," reasonable men may differ about the intent of Congress in the 1890s. What is clear is that since then, Congress has never overruled a decision that failed the price theory test. With the Celler Amendment, it did overrule *Columbia Steel* (1948),[13] which, on economic grounds, surely qualifies as a good decision.

Why the United States got antitrust instead of a strong socialist movement is a question for students of intellectual history. We did adopt antitrust, and it has proved to be an astoundingly effective tranquilizer. Even professional economists have been known to feel better about the state of the nation when they were able to conclude that antitrust has reduced the four-firm concentration ratio in major industries.

A loss of popular faith in antitrust may well have serious consequences if it ever happens. That danger is not yet on the horizon. A more immediate crisis is likely to result from the present administration's efforts to change course abruptly. A few more uncontested mergers on the scale of Gulf-Socal and the country will have a new and tougher merger law.

In short, I do not believe that there is an antitrust paradox, within Bork's meaning. Over the years, the courts have interpreted the vague clauses of the antitrust laws in ways that have found favor with Congress. To me, the real paradox is why economists in the United States have been such staunch friends of the policy—at least, until recently. The best explanation that I can offer is that in our impressionable early years, we come under

---

[12]I believe that the most detailed examinations of the origins of the Sherman Act support the above view. William Letwin, *Law and Economic Policy in America* (1965), pp. 71–77; and H. B. Thorelli, *The Federal Antitrust Policy* (1954), pp. 108–27. For a similar, though not identical, view of the origins of antitrust, see M. A. Adelman, "An Economist Looks at the Sherman Act," 27 *Proceedings of the American Bar Association Section of Antitrust Law* 32 (1965).

[13]*United States v. Columbia Steel Co. et al.*, 334 U.S. 495 (1948).

the same influences as future congressmen and federal judges. I recall the shock when, fresh from the University of Chicago of Henry Simons, I first met European economists who regarded antitrust as a curious—though probably harmless—bit of American folly. With the zeal of the young believer, I even tried to persuade the heathen to read *A Positive Program for Laissez Faire*. I think that Bork will agree that shaking off these early influences has not been easy.

It is right that we should fight against the misuse (even downright prostitution) of economics in antitrust litigation and to expose the anticonsumer consequences of much of present policy. As D. H. Robertson used to remind us, if economists do not speak up for economic efficiency, nobody will. However, I always took this caution to mean that, as a good citizen, I should share my learning and wisdom—not as a call to become a missionary on behalf of Pareto optimality. In antitrust work, our strictly professional role ends when the cost-benefit analysis of a proposed course of conduct has been finished.

Back to basics. The popularity of antitrust is based on nothing more profound than fear of great corporate size and the rich, powerful, and often remote people who occupy high corporate office. (Antitrust is not unique in this respect.) No congressman was ever frightened by a small firm with a large market share. Until this fear of bigness is shown to be mostly groundless—or somehow fades away—no radical revision of antitrust to make it more efficient will be possible. Or, I will argue, even desirable. Incremental improvements that educate should be the goal. Reform of antitrust is likely to be difficult precisely because the stakes are so small; that is, there can be no big payoff comparable to that associated with deregulation of the airlines to get the ball rolling.

I doubt that many congressmen who had the benefit of Dewey's instruction would endorse many of Bork's recommendations. Antitrust may not make much difference to substance, but it makes a great deal of difference to appearances. For example, if a congressman believes Dewey, he will certainly conclude that taking a hard line against conglomerate mergers is a wonderfully cheap way of gaining the approval of a great many people including editorial writers, political science professors, and not a few economists.

At the close of the industrial organization course, I used to ask the class to speculate on the economic and political consequences of repealing the antitrust laws. I still like the economic part of the question, but no longer believe that the political part has pedagogical value. Antitrust is simply too much of a sacred cow in American politics. At present, there is not much point in constructing scenarios about what would happen if the national consensus which supports it should disappear.

Justice Douglas believed that the country's only choice was between his version of antitrust and some detestable kind of state socialism. I am never entirely free of the fear that he could be right. De Tocqueville chided the middle classes of nineteenth-century France for their contemptuous anticlericalism, observing that the excesses of the Great Revolution should have taught them the utility, if not the truth, of religion. I no longer believe that anybody—not even Bork—can construct a valid case for antitrust from price theory. Is not the reason really very simple? On the assumption that property rights are specified, price theory rigorously applied always underlines the beneficent consequences of freedom of contract; people ascend to higher indifference curves by engaging in exchange. No matter how we sugarcoat it, antitrust is a set of restrictions on freedom of contract.[14]

My disbelief in antitrust as a policy of consumer protection is now virtually complete. The qualifying adverb is applied only because some recent antitrust attacks on the restrictive practices of state and local governments at long last promise some consumer benefits.[15] But since I can easily imagine economic policies far worse than antitrust, I am glad that it is there. Far better that my countrymen should seek reassurance in stable or declining industry-concentration ratios than in state-owned monopolies or indicative economic planning. Whatever its truth content, antitrust is the kind of undemanding secular religion that an agnostic like myself can live with.

[14]Dominick Armentano has been reminding us of this truth for quite a few years, notably in *Antitrust and Monopoly* (1982).

[15]Notably *City of Lafayette v. Louisiana Power & Light Co.,* 435 U.S. 389 (1978).

8.

Antitrust and Its Alternatives: A Compleat Guide to the Welfare Tradeoffs

"To see what is in front of one's nose needs a constant struggle."

—*attributed to George Orwell*

HIS STUDY was prompted by an experience at one of Dean Henry Manne's conferences on antitrust in the late 1970s. Manne believed that law in general and antitrust law in particular could be improved by demonstrating to judges and lawyers the relevance of price theory to the issues before them. The guest list of a Manne conference was invariably a distinguished one. However, it always had a distinctly libertarian and social conservative cast. My recollection is that Manne never invested his time or conference budgets in trying to convert socialists or populists or providing them with a forum. The alliance between libertarians and social conservatives in the United States is, of course, an historical accident. Social conservatives generally come to esteem any set of economic arrangements that they have gotten used to and that provides comfortable structure to their lives. To libertarians, economic freedom is an essential part of personal freedom—which is the supreme value.

At the Manne conference, I went public for the first time with my total agnosticism concerning the economic benefits imputed to antitrust. I questioned whether any case for the policy could be constructed from basic

Reprinted from Ronald E. Grieson, ed., *Antitrust and Regulation* (Lexington, Mass.: Lexington Books, 1986). For their generous (and often exacting) attention to earlier drafts of this paper, I would like to thank my colleagues, Bruce Bassett, Nicholas Economides, and William Vickrey.

price theory and its implicit welfare tests. Given the character of a Manne audience, I expected at least a sympathetic hearing for my position. Instead, the reception was one of impatient skepticism. Discussion soon turned to other matters. I could only conclude that, while the members of the audience may have had plenty of grievances against real world antitrust (and they certainly did), the Sherman Act embodied an ideal that still commanded their allegiance. In any event, it was clear that if a group of economists and lawyers selected by Henry Manne did not find my case persuasive, I must be doing something wrong.

The case against antitrust as a promoter of economic welfare that I then offered was (I think) a good one. It had been slowly developed and frequently argued over a period of twenty-five years. However, the case was eclectic, having been constructed from arguments drawn from the diverse sources of price theory, empirical studies, business history, and casual empiricism. And being eclectic, the case lacked a sharp focus. I had made the mistake of overlooking Paul Samuelson's warning that nobody takes an economist seriously until he puts his ideas into a theory. So, drawing heavily on what I had learned in twenty years of association with William Vickrey, I set out to build one.

When the work was done, I had a model that confirmed what I had suspected from the start—that antitrust in the form favored by its most fervent supporters, e.g., Walter Adams and the late Justice William Douglas, was an engine for creating excess capacity. What I had not anticipated was the magnitude of the welfare loss such a policy might impose or the certainty with which the loss would be imposed. Real world antitrust is still a far cry from the ideal of Adams and Douglas, though until the Reagan presidency it was moving steadily closer. Measuring the welfare cost of real world antitrust will remain, for as far into the future as we can presume to see, a difficult and possibly an intractable empirical problem. The claim that I make for the "economic theory of antitrust" offered below is that, to date, it is the only game in town—the only alternative to welfare judgments about antitrust based on casual empiricism or a selection of case studies drawn from different decades. To change the metaphor, as old Bill said to the terrified recruit in no-man's-land in the most famous cartoon of World War I, if you know a better 'ole, go to it.

An Uncertain Foundation

MOST ECONOMISTS believe that the tools of price theory can be used to throw light on the welfare effects of antitrust rules that restrict freedom of contract. We could hardly believe otherwise and retain our self-respect. However, most economists also seem to believe that when these tools are properly employed, it will be found that at least some antitrust rules serve to increase economic welfare. This conviction survives despite the fact that over the last thirty-five years many of the arguments long used to justify antitrust rules have been discredited and no new ones have been advanced.[1] True, many of the economists and lawyers who most closely follow antitrust in action now view it with a mixture of exasperation, regret, and even outright contempt. But, for almost every critic, a spark of hope remains. According to an argument much favored by economists, what is needed is the correct understanding and use of price theory—especially by federal judges. For their part, lawyers have proved to be surprisingly receptive to this argument—probably because they have concluded that, in the strange and often unpredictable world of antitrust, they need all the help they can get.

Possibly a psychiatrist well versed in economics and American history could offer some interesting insights into the need of American economists to believe in at least the possibility of doing good through antitrust. They might, for example, be able to throw some light on why we jeopardize our professional standing with colleagues by appearing to speak approvingly of either big business or big government. Still, it is not necessary to call in psychiatry to make a prima facie case that the faith in the economic possibilities of antitrust may have no very firm foundation. We can readily cite reasons for doubting that it is possible to devise a set of antitrust rules that creates more economic welfare than it destroys—even under the most favorable circumstances that can reasonably be imagined.

[1]M. A. Adelman, "The Measurement of Industrial Concentration," 33 *Rev. Econ. Stat.* 269 (1951); D. T. Armentano, *Antitrust and Monopoly: Anatomy of a Policy Failure* (1982); Peter Asch and Joseph Seneca, "Is Collusion Profitable?" 58 *Rev. Econ. Stat.* 1 (1976); William J. Baumol, James C. Panzar, and Robert D. Willig, *Contestable Markets and the Theory of Industry Structure* (1982); Robert H. Bork, *The Antitrust Paradox: A Policy at War with Itself* (1978); Ward S. Bowman, Jr., "Tying Arrangements and the Leverage Problem," 67 *Yale L.J.* 19 (1957); Yale Brozen, *Concentration, Mergers, and Public Policy* (1982); Donald Dewey, "Information, Entry, and Welfare: The Case for Collusion," 63 *Am. Econ. Rev.* 69 (1979); Kenneth G. Elzinga and William Breit, *The Antitrust Penalties: A Study in Law And Economics* (1976); John McGee, *In Defense of Industrial Concentration* (1971); John Moore and G. Warren Nutter, "A Theory of Competition," 19 *J. Law Econ.* 39 (1976); Richard A. Posner, *Antitrust Law: An Economic Perspective* (1976); George B. Richardson, "The Theory of Restrictive Trade Practices," 17 *Oxford Econ. Papers* 432 (1965); Joseph E. Stiglitz, "Potential Competition May Reduce Welfare," 71 *Am. Econ. Rev.* 184 (1981); L. G. Telser, "Cutthroat Competition and the Long Purse," 9 *J. Law Econ.* 259 (1966); B. S. Yamey, *The Economics of Resale Price Maintenance* (1954).

One reason has already been mentioned. In recent years, economists have had far more success in using price theory to discredit antitrust rules than to justify them. Four other reasons deserve mention here.

First, we have ancient ancestral warnings against trying to do good by imposing restrictions on freedom of contract. Adam Smith contemptuously likened the eighteenth century forerunner of antitrust—laws against forestalling, engrossing, and regrating—to laws against witchcraft.[2] And in the 1890s, most American economists received the new Sherman Act with hostility or indifference.[3] Considering the enormous volume of writing on antitrust, it is surprising that no study has yet traced the steps by which American economists came to accept the policy and assist in its elevation to the status of sacred cow in American law and politics. My own suspicion is that this conversion was due more to the conclusion that antitrust was here to stay than to any enlightenment traceable to theoretical or empirical work.

Second, there is an unmistakable void in the very considerable literature on "welfare economics" that should give us pause. The possibilities of using taxes, subsidies, and marginal cost pricing to increase economic welfare are debated at great length in this literature. The possibility of using antitrust rules to advance this good cause is scarcely ever mentioned.[4]

Third, at least until recently, faith in the economic possibilities of antitrust has been a particularly American phenomenon. Thus, the English observer A. D. Neale, after his careful look at American antitrust, concluded that, while the policy was undoubtedly a political success in this country, it imposed economic costs that the British economy could not afford.[5] The disdain of Joseph Shumpeter for the policy—his long residence in this country notwithstanding—is well known.[6]

Finally, we have the uncomfortable truth that the "naive" case for antitrust is too shoddy to be taken seriously. This is the case that explicitly or implicitly (1) equates a high concentration ratio and/or collusion in an industry with "monopoly power," (2) assumes that measures that increase the number of viable firms and/or reduce collusion make an industry "more

---

[2]Adam Smith, *The Wealth of Nations,* Mod. Lib. ed. (1937), p. 501.

[3]See, for example, William Letwin, "Congress and the Sherman Antitrust Law, 1887–1890," 23 *U. Chicago Law Rev.* 221 (1956); or H. B. Thorelli, *The Federal Antitrust Policy* (1954), pp. 108–127.

[4]See, for example, I. M. D. Little, *A Critique of Welfare Economics,* 2nd ed., (1957); or E. J. Mishan, *Welfare Economics: Five Introductory Essays,* 2d ed., (1969).

[5]Alan D. Neale, *The Antitrust Laws of the United States of America,* 2d ed. (1970), pp. 478–93.

[6]See, for example, Joseph Schumpeter, *Capitalism, Socialism, and Democracy,* 3d ed. (1950), pp. 87–106.

competitive," and (3) assumes that an increase in competition must lead to an increase in economic welfare.

Look closely at this argument. Point (1) assumes a tie between industrial concentration and/or collusion that is a matter for empirical study. Point (2) assumes the truth of point (1) and, on this assumption, becomes a tautology. Point (3), again, assumes that which must be proved. While economic welfare may be difficult to measure, in economic analysis the meaning of the term is unambiguous. So also is the test by which the impact of an antitrust rule on economic welfare is to be evaluated. There is no increase in economic welfare unless, as a result of the rule's use, people who gain would in principle be able fully to compensate those who lose and still be better off themselves.[7] The whole point of the exercise that follows is to try to assess the impact on economic welfare of several alternative ways of organizing the economy—one of which is antitrust.

Clearly there is no self-evident reason for presuming that whatever increases competition (however defined) must also increase economic welfare. Has not virtually every basic theory book published in the last forty years contained the diagrams taken from Joan Robinson[8] and Edward Chamberlin[9] that show how free entry in an imperfectly competitive market leads to the "wastes of excess capacity"? The Chicagoans have often complained that textbook treatments of imperfect competition are highly misleading. This is true enough. But the textbooks mislead, not because they contain gross errors of logic, but because they fail to make clear what must be assumed before imperfect competition necessarily leads to excess capacity.[10]

In this paper we shall take up the challenge implicit in much of the popular and professional literature on antitrust: to identify the conditions that must be met before antitrust is, on welfare grounds, preferable to its alternatives.[11] To respond to this challenge, it is not necessary to believe that the maximization of economic welfare is the only proper goal of an-

---

[7] As usually formulated, an increase in economic welfare does not require that compensation actually be paid to losers—only that it could be paid out of the gains of the winners from a rule change. The compensation test seems originally to have been suggested as a way of getting policy makers to think twice about rule changes whose advocates promise economic benefits. John R. Hicks, "The Foundations of Welfare Economics," 49 *Econ. J.* 696, 711–12 (1939).

[8] Joan Robinson, *The Economics of Imperfect Competition* (1933).

[9] Edward Chamberlin, *The Theory of Monopolistic Competition* (1933).

[10] Harold Demsetz, "The Welfare and Empirical Implications of Monopolistic Competition," 74 *Econ. J.* 622 (1964); Donald Dewey, *The Theory of Imperfect Competition: A Radical Reconstruction* (1969), pp. 60–86.

[11] For the pioneer effort to estimate antitrust tradeoffs, see Oliver Williamason, "Economies as an Antitrust Defense," 58 *Am. Econ. Rev.* 18 (1968).

titrust or that price theory is the only acceptable organon for estimating
the welfare impact of antitrust rules. One need only believe that no antitrust rule should be allowed to escape the scrutiny of price theory (and the
compensation test).

Four Policy Alternatives

LET US begin with fundamentals. Antitrust is good or bad only in relation to something else. The leading alternatives in their purest form—as
Max Weber's ideal types[12]—are three: (1) regulated monopoly with marginal cost pricing (henceforth called "regulation") that may require a sub-
sidy; (2) laissez-faire that leads to multiplant firms or cartels which practice
limit pricing (henceforth called "laissez-faire"); and (3) totally unregulated
monopoly completely protected by Law or Nature (henceforth called
"monopoly").

We shall take "ideal" antitrust (ideal only in the Weberian sense) to be
a policy that has two main goals. First, it seeks the maximum number of
viable firms in an industry that can be achieved without imposing a limit
to internal growth of firms. This it does by banning mergers among viable
firms in the industry[13] and outlawing predatory and exclusionary pricing.
Second, ideal antitrust seeks to suppress collusion. In short, our "ideal"
antitrust has goals virtually identical to those that the late Justice Douglas ·
endeavored to embed in the law in his many antitrust opinions.

Some friends of antitrust would prefer to say that these two goals are
not ends in themselves but merely the means by which economic welfare
can be increased. I will not stop to quarrel with the value judgment that
economic welfare ought to be the main concern of antitrust. No doubt
many federal judges and most Federal Trade Commissioners believe that,
in some rough and ready way, they promote this larger end by preserving
viable firms and suppressing collusion. These considerations do not alter
the fact that, in the routine administration of antitrust, the preservation of
viable firms and the suppression of collusion are treated as ends in themselves—or, at any rate, as ends mandated by the policy that are now almost beyond question. Price-fixing agreements have long been illegal per

[12]Max Weber, *The Theory of Social and Economic Organization*, A. R. Henderson and Talcott
Parsons, trans. (1947), pp. 79–102.

[13]That the concern of antitrust has long been not with the efficiency of firms but with their
viability is easily documented. Since *International Shoe Co. v. F.T.C.*, 280 U.S. 291 (1930),
a showing that a firm is likely to fail unless allowed to merge has been the only complete
defense against the government's effort to prevent a merger that would otherwise violate
section 7 of the Clayton Act.

se. Since *Brown Shoe* (1963),[14] mergers that are thought to reduce the number of "healthy" competitors might as well be. Admittedly, the Reagan administration has been somewhat softer on mergers than its predecessors; it remains to be seen whether this policy revision will be accepted by Congress or retained by future administrations.

In this exercise, we are not concerned with what the goals of antitrust ought to be nor will we try to discover what Congress "really" hoped to accomplish by the Sherman Act in 1890. Rather, relying on the venerable maxim that men must be presumed to intend the consequences of their acts, we infer the major goals of antitrust from its most obvious consequences.

Each of the above four organizational alternatives is, of course, dependent upon the observance of legal rules that have enforcement costs. In the first instance, however, we shall examine the comparative welfare merits of antitrust and its rivals on the premise that these costs are null.

A Method for Comparing Welfare Tradeoffs

THE CONVENTIONAL models of monopoly, marginal cost pricing (with subsidies to decreasing cost industries if necessary), and limit pricing are well known and require no detailed description here.[15] But we need a model of "competition." When the number of firms that antitrust can sustain in the market is relatively small, the model of perfect competition is obviously inappropriate. The model of competition that we shall use to discern the impact on welfare of the market structure that antitrust presumably seeks to create is "Cournot with cost curves."[16]

This model is admirably suited to our purposes. It is totally free of collusion to restrict output and of pricing to intimidate rivals. Each firm, in selecting its rate of output, takes the outputs of all other firms in the industry as given. Some economists distrust the results of any analysis based upon the Cournot model because it assumes that each firm knows the industry demand function, the outputs of all rival firms, and never learns from experience that any change in its own output will cause other firms

---

[14]*United States v. Brown Shoe Co.*, 370, U.S. 294 (1963).

[15]On the details of limit pricing, see Donald Dewey, *Microeconomics: The Analysis of Prices and Markets* (1975), pp. 141–54; Darius W. Gaskins, "Dynamic Limit Pricing: Optimal Pricing under Threat of Entry," 3 *J. Econ. Theory* 306 (1971); and B. P. Pashigian, "Limit Price and the Market Share of the Leading Firm," 16 *J. Ind. Econ.* 165 (1968).

[16]In using the Cournot model with cost curves as a proxy for "competition," I also have the comfort of knowing that I am in highly respectable company. See William Novshek and Hugo Sonnenschein, "Cournot and Walras Equilibrium," 19 *J. Econ. Theory* 223 (1978).

to change their outputs.[17] While this criticism states a virtually obvious truth, it does not tell against the use of the Cournot model as a proxy, especially as its properties have been elaborated by William Vickrey.

Some years ago, in investigating the behavior of the firm under conditions of uncertainty, Vickrey obtained a quite remarkable result.[18] He considered the case where sellers in an imperfectly competitive market began production in near total ignorance. They do not know the demand for the product nor do they even know of one another's existence. A seller's only means of gaining information is by varying output during some time period, tabulating the results, and constructing a statistical demand function. Vickrey assumed that a seller would use the derived demand function for a time and then vary output again to construct a new one. No information can be exchanged among sellers. It was Vickrey's achievement to show that, on these assumptions, the industry will converge to the same price and output as in a static Cournot equilibrium containing the same number of sellers. In view of this extension of the Cournot model to noncollusive pricing under conditions of uncertainty, it would be almost gratuitous to ask for a better proxy for the "competition" sought by real world antitrust.

Models of imperfect competition may be indispensible in any analysis of the welfare effects of antitrust and its alternatives. Unhappily, such models are not easy to describe mathematically since the demand function of each firm changes every time another firm enters or leaves the industry. The Cournot model is no exception. To make the problem tractable, we shall resort to the diplomat's technique of best case and worse case analysis and to elementary probability theory. That is, we shall first estimate the maximum and minimum impacts on economic welfare of shifting to antitrust from "something else." We shall then assign a probability distribution to the possible welfare outcomes that lie within these upper and lower bounds. We do so with the aid of three additional assumptions.

ASSUMPTION A1. All firms in the industry have identical cost functions and hence are replicates of one another; any proposition about one firm applies to all firms.

ASSUMPTION A2. The industry's demand function is linear and can be written as $p = a - bx(a > b > 0)$ where p denotes price and x output.

[17]A. A. Cournot, *Recherches sur les principes mathématiques de la théorie des richesses* (1838); translated by N. T. Bacon as *Researches into the Mathematical Principles of the Theory of Wealth* (1897).
[18]William S. Vickrey, *Microstatics* (1964), pp. 304–9.

Later on, we shall consider the consequences of relaxing this assumption of linearity. For the present, it will suffice to note that the principal requirement of a demand curve is that it describes a total revenue function that has a maximum. A linear demand curve satisfies this test. Since there is no obvious reason for prefering nonlinearity to linearity, we shall use it and so avoid the often excruciating algebraic complexities associated with operations involving nonlinear demand curves.

ASSUMPTION A3. At every output in the firm, marginal cost is either zero or infinity.

This last assumption—possibly rather strange on first meeting—immensely simplified our analysis in two ways. (Indeed, without it, a comparison of the economic consequences of antitrust with those of its alternatives would be impossible.)

First, assumption A3 means that we need concern ourselves with only two possible unit cost curves. The first is the rectangular hyperbola ZZ' in figure 8.2. With the aid of ZZ' in figure 8.2, we shall be able to measure the welfare impact of antitrust in the worst case, i.e., under the most unfavorable conditions. The second unit cost curve is the fishhook curve ZZ' in figure 8.3. This curve will allow us to measure the welfare impact of antitrust in the best case.[19]

Let us be clear that the unit cost curves ZZ' of figures 8.2 and 8.3 are "limit cases." Their usefulness in our analysis is not affected by the probability, amounting to a virtual certainty, that they are nowhere exactly reproduced in the real world. For our purposes it is enough that they establish the limits within which any real world curve of unit cost must fall.

Used in conjunction with an industry demand curve that is linear, the assumption that, at every output, marginal cost in the firm is either zero or infinity makes possible the second essential simplification in our analysis. It allows us to identify the equilibrium demand function for the individual firm when the industry operates under antitrust.

The firm will not produce an output at which marginal cost is infinite; therefore, in n-firm equilibrium, each firm produces an output at which marginal cost is zero. And it is a property of the linear Cournot model that, when marginal cost is zero, each firm in n-firm equilibrium believes its demand function to be of the form $p = [2a/(n + 1)] - bx$.[20] For our

---

[19]For evidence that some unit cost curves of the real world really do approximate the fishhook curve of figure 8.3, see William J. Eiteman and Glenn E. Guthrie, "The Shape of the Average Cost Curve," 42 *Am. Econ. Rev.* 832 (1952).

[20]In Cournot equilibrium, when the aggregate demand function is of the form $p = a - bx$, the equilibrium demand function of a single seller is

purposes, an *n*-firm equilibrium exists when: (1) with *n* firms, price is not less than unit cost, and (2) with *n* + 1 firms, price would be less than unit cost. Once we know the demand function for a firm in *n*-firm equilibrium under antitrust, we can make the computations necessary for a comparison of economic welfare merits of antitrust and its alternatives. For example, if under antitrust, each firm always produces where marginal cost is zero

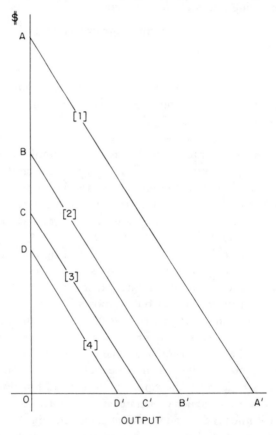

FIGURE 8.1

$$p = \frac{(n + 1)m + 2(a - m)}{n + 1} - bx \qquad 8.4$$

where *n* denotes number of sellers and *m* denotes marginal cost (or marginal revenue).
When *m* = 0, eq. 8.4 can be rewritten as

$$p = \frac{2a}{n + 1} - bx \qquad 8.4a$$

and its demand function is of the form $p = [2a/(n + 1)] - bx$, then whatever the value taken by n, in n-firm equilibrium price is always equal to $a/(n + 1)$.

Figure 8.1 depicts a set of equilibrium demand functions for various equilibrium n's on the assumption that marginal cost is zero. Thus AA' is the demand cureve for each firm when $n = 1$. BB' is the equilibrium demand curve for each firm when $n = 2$, etc. A most convenient feature of the Cournot model with a linear demand curve is, of course, that while the demand curve will change for each firm as n changes, the slope of the firm's demand curve does not change.

Antitrust in the Worst Case

THE WORST case view of antitrust when the number of firms is four is given by figure 8.2. (Resort to geometry requires us to assign a numerical value to n and $n = 4$ is as good as any.) EG (and EG') is the industry demand curve. BI is its own demand curve as perceived by each of the

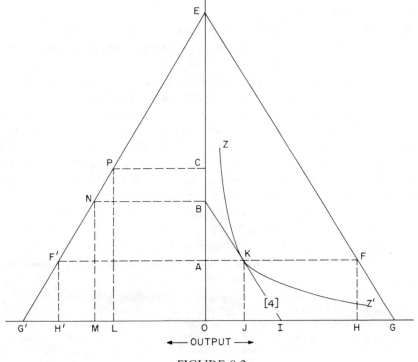

FIGURE 8.2

four firms. The unit cost curve of each firm is ZZ'. Why does figure 8.2 depict the worst case of 4-firm equilibrium under antitrust? Simply because it shows the maximum amount of excess capacity waste that is consistent with 4-firm equilibrium.

A firm does not produce on the inelastic segment of its demand curve. Thus, in figure 8.2 OJ is greatest possible output per firm in 4-firm equilibrium. The rectangular hyperbola ZZ' is the limit case of so-called "natural monopoly." Thus, three of the four firms are redundant and excess capacity waste is given by $JHFK$ in figure 8.2. If the production of industry output OH were any more wasteful, at least one firm would leave the industry.

And the welfare gain of antitrust in the worst case? If antitrust is here substituted for monopoly, price falls from OC to OA in figure 8.2; and industry output increases from OL to OH'. The additional output (which is LH') adds to economic welfare the area $H'F'PL$ in figure 8.2. However, the cost of this additional output is $JKFH$; this is because the shift to antitrust has caused the entry of three more firms, each with the unit cost curve ZZ'. Thus, in the worst case, the *net* gain in economic welfare resulting from the substitution of antitrust for monopoly is the area H' F' PL minus the $JKFH$ in figure 8.2. Close inspection of figure 8.2 will show what will be given a mathematical proof later: that the latter area exceeds the former. Hence, in the worst case, an antitrust action that replaces monopoly with 4-firm equilibrium leads to a net loss of economic welfare.

If antitrust is substituted for laissez-faire (with limit pricing), price falls from OB to OA in figure 8.2 and industry output increases from OM to OH'.[21] The additional output (which is MH) adds to economic welfare the area $H'F'NM$ in figure 8.2. The cost of this additional output is again the area $JKFH$. Close inspection of figure 8.2 will show that the area $JKFH$ is greater than the area $H'F'NM$; so that the substitution of 4-firm equilibrium under antitrust for laissez-faire causes a net reduction in economic welfare. This, too, will be given a formal proof later on.

Finally, in the worst case, let antitrust be substituted for ideal (subsidized) regulation. In figure 8.2, the substitution will cause price to rise from zero to OA and output to fall from OG to OH. This reduction in output will cause economic welfare to fall by the amount GFH. However,

---

[21]In figures 8.2 and 8.3, let the price charged by a sole producer in the market be OB and his output OM (or BN). Here the "unused" portion of the industry demand curve EG is the segment NG'. This gives the potential entrant the demand curve BI. Faced with this demand curve, the potential entrant can enter and break even by producing OJ. Therefore, assuming that the sole producer wishes to discourage entrants, he must charge a price that is below the upper limit OB and so put the demand curve for a potential entrant below BI.

because three more firms enter the industry under antitrust (each with the unit cost curve ZZ'), total cost does not fall; it increases by the amount *JKFH*. Thus, in the worst case, the net loss of economic welfare when antitrust is substituted for ideal regulation is the sum of the areas $GF'\,H'$ and *JKFH* in figure 8.2.

Our analysis shows that, if antitrust can create only four viable firms, then, in the worst case, it is the worst possible choice. Even monopoly is better. However, a close look at figure 8.2 will reveal that, while antitrust in the worst case always creates less economic welfare than regulation, antitrust—even at its worst—is an improvement on monopoly when n is great enough.

In figure 8.2 suppose the curve of unit cost ZZ' to move downward toward the origin. As this happens, additional firms enter, price falls, and the consumer surplus created by antitrust increases. At the same time, the industry's total cost decreases and, as n goes to infinity, total cost goes to zero. Thus, there must exist a set of n's for which, even in the worst case, antitrust is preferable to monopoly. (We shall presently show that antitrust is always better than monopoly when $n > 6$.) From figure 8.2 it is not immediately clear whether antitrust is ever preferable to laissez-faire. We consider this problem later. In worst case analysis, regulation remains the best of the alternatives so long as n is a finite number.

Antitrust in the Best Case

NOW CONSIDER the best case view of antitrust when the equilibrium number of firms is four.[22] This view is given by figure 3. Once again EG (and EG') is the industry demand curve. Again BI is the demand curve as perceived by each of the four firms. Now the unit cost curve is given by the fish hook curve ZZ' in figure 8.3.

In figure 8.3, price is OA and output per firm is OJ under antitrust— the same as in figure 8.2. But in this best case antitrust, there is no excess

---

[22]To simplify the presentation, in figures 8.2 and 8.3 the unit cost curve ZZ' has been drawn tangent to the demand curve BI at point K; that is, our choice of geometry has insured that the entry of the fourth firm exactly eliminates all monopoly rent (usually called "profit"). An n-firm equilibrium with positive profit for all firms is, of course, possible—provided that the aggregate profit is not great enough to draw an additional firm into the industry.

Let s denote total sales revenue per firm, t total cost per firm and r the profit-sales ratio. Then $r = (s - t)/s$. It can be shown (though we will not stop to do so) that in n-firm equilibrium in a Cournot model the maximum value that r can take must be less than $[1 - (n + 1)^2/(n + 2)^2]$. The technique for locating the upper bound for r in an oligopoly model that allows free entry is described and illustrated in chapter 5.

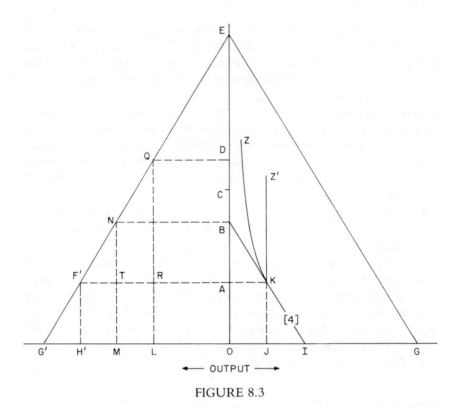

FIGURE 8.3

capacity waste; each of the four firms produces at the minimum point on its unit cost curve *ZZ'*. (*K* designates this minimum point). One cannot improve upon perfection.

If the industry were organized as monopoly (either through a cartel or multiplant firm), the monopolist's long-run marginal cost would approximate OA (or JK) in figure 8.3. For marginal cost is equal to *OA* for all multiples of output *OJ*. Under best case antitrust, industry output is *OH'*. Under monopoly, industry output is *OH/2* or *OL* and price is *OD*. The substitution of antitrust for monopoly now leads to additional output *LH'*. Thus the net gain in economic welfare from substituting antitrust for monopoly is here the triangle *F'QR* in figure 8.3. To repeat, best case antitrust is best because its substitution for something else creates no excess capacity waste.

In figure 8.3, the substitution of antitrust for laissez-faire produces a net gain in economic welfare equal to the triangle *F'NT*. Note that, in the best case, the welfare impact of antitrust is the same as that of regulation (with marginal cost pricing). In figure 8.3, *OA* approximates the long-run marginal cost to which regulators will presumably equate price. For *OA* remains minimum attainable unit cost as production units (firms or plants) are added or dropped.

In the best case (figure 8.3), where antitrust leads to no excess capacity waste, it is always preferable to both monopoly and laissez-faire. And here it is just as good as regulation leading to the same price and output.

Probable Tradeoffs

THE ECONOMIC import of figures 8.2 and 8.3 can now be generalized for *n*-firm equilibrium for any industry demand function of the form

$$p = a - bx(a > b > 0).$$

Suppose that we are given one additional bit of information: the equilibrium number of firms that will emerge when the industry operates under antitrust, i.e., the value of *n*. It is now possible to make some quite specific statements about the net gain (or loss) in economic welfare when antitrust is substituted for one of its alternatives.

Assume that in this *n*-firm equilibrium we have the hyperbolic curve of unit cost (*ZZ′* figure 8.2) that makes possible worst case antitrust. We can easily reckon, for worst case antitrust, all of the following: price, total output, total revenue, and excess capacity waste.

We can go further. Our information also allows us to reckon all of the above values for our three alternatives to worst case antitrust: regulation (with marginal cost pricing), laissez-faire (with limit pricing), and monopoly. Let us be clear that the substitution of worst case antitrust for these three alternatives does not affect the industry's demand curve or the unit cost curve of the individual production unit (plant or firm). Hence, any change in economic welfare resulting from the substitution can be imputed entirely to the change in legal rules. When the necessary algebraic operations have been performed, the results are those entered in table 8.1.

Similar calculations can be made for the industry on the assumption that each firm has the fish hook curve of unit cost (*ZZ′* in figure 8.3) that makes possible best case antitrust. When they are made, the results are those entered in table 8.2.

From the information in tables 8.1 and 8.2, we can determine the net welfare gain (or loss) obtainable by substituting antitrust for each of its alternatives first on worst case assumptions and then on best case assumptions. We use the notation set forth in table 8.3.

In this notation, M_n denotes the net change in economic welfare that

TABLE 8.1. Antitrust: Worst Case

	Antitrust	Regulation (mc pricing)	Laissez-Faire (limit pricing)-	Monopoly
Price	$\dfrac{a}{(n+1)}$	0	$\dfrac{2a}{(n+1)}$	$\dfrac{a}{2}$
Output	$\dfrac{na}{b(n+1)}$	$\dfrac{a}{b}$	$\dfrac{a(n-1)}{b(n+1)}$	$\dfrac{a}{2b}$
Total revenue	$\dfrac{na^2}{b(n+1)^2}$	0	$\dfrac{2a^2(n-1)}{b(n+1)^2}$	$\dfrac{a^2}{4b}$
Total cost	$\dfrac{na^2}{b(n+1)^2}$	$\dfrac{a^2}{b(n+1)^2}$	$\dfrac{a^2}{b(n+1)^2}$	$\dfrac{a^2}{b(n+1)^2}$
Excess capacity waste	$\dfrac{(n-1)a^2}{b(n+1)^2}$	0	0	0

TABLE 8.2. Antitrust: Best Case

	Antitrust	Regulation (mc pricing)	Laissez-Faire (limit pricing)	Monopoly
Price	$\dfrac{a}{(n+1)}$	$\dfrac{a}{(n+1)}$	$\dfrac{2a}{(n+1)}$	$\dfrac{a(n+2)}{2(n+1)}$
Output	$\dfrac{na}{b(n+1)}$	$\dfrac{na}{b(n+1)}$	$\dfrac{n-1}{b(n+1)}$	$\dfrac{na}{2b(n+1)}$
Total revenue	$\dfrac{na^2}{b(n+1)^2}$	$\dfrac{na^2}{b(n+1)^2}$	$\dfrac{2a^2(n-1)}{b(n+1)^2}$	$\dfrac{a^2n(n+2)}{4b(n+1)^2}$
Total cost	$\dfrac{na^2}{b(n+1)^2}$	$\dfrac{na^2}{b(n+1)^2}$	$\dfrac{a^2(n-1)}{b(n+1)^2}$	$\dfrac{na^2}{2b(n+1)^2}$
Excess capacity waste	0	0	0	0

occurs when antitrust is substituted for monopoly (and n-firm equilibrium results). Suppose that we wish to find Min M_n—the value for M_n when this substitution is made in the worst case. This shift will cause industry output to increase, but it will also cause excess capacity to appear. Specifically, in the worst case, replacing monopoly with antitrust will cause output to increase from $a/2b$ to $na/b(n+1)$. The increase in economic welfare from this additional output is given by:

TABLE 8.3. Notation for Probable Tradeoffs

M_n = the net welfare change when antitrust replaces monopoly
L_n = the net welfare change when antitrust replaces laissez-faire
R_n = the next welfare change when antitrust replaces regulation
Max M_n = maximum value of M_n consistent with n-firm equilibrium
Min M_n = minimum value of M_n consistent with n-firm equilibrium
Max L_n = maximum value of L_n consistent with n-firm equilibrium
Min L_n = minimum value of L_n consistent with n-firm equilibrium
Max R_n = maximum value of R_n consistent with n-firm equilibrium
Min R_n = minimum value of R_n consistent with n-firm equilibrium

$$\int_{a/2b}^{na/b(n+1)} (a - bx)dx$$

Recall that the industry's demand function is $p = a - bx$, where p denotes price and x denotes output.

The cost of the additional output is given by:

$$(n - 1)a^2/b(n + 1)^2$$

Thus,

$$\text{Min}_n = \int_{a/2b}^{na/b(n+1)} (a - bx)dx - \frac{(n - 1)a^2}{b(n + 1)^2} \tag{8.1}$$

Integrating and simplifying, we get

$$\text{Min } M_n = \frac{a^2(n^2 - 6n + 5)}{8b(n + 1)^2} \tag{8.2}$$

Using information tabulated in table 8.1, we can go on to find the values of Min L_n and Min R_n. Using the information tabulated in table 8.2, we can find the values of Max M_n, Max L_n and Max R_n. The results are summarized in table 8.4. We note again that in best case antitrust, there is no excess capacity waste; hence, the maximum values for M_n, L_n and R_n are equal to the changes in consumer surplus that result when antitrust replaces monopoly, laissez-faire, and regulation respectively.

As table 8.1 shows, when antitrust is substituted for something else,

TABLE 8.4. Net Welfare Change When Antitrust Replaces Various Alternatives

	Regulation (mc pricing)	Laissez-Faire (limit pricing)	Monopoly
Best case	Max R_n	Max L_n	Max M_n
	0	$\dfrac{a^2}{2b(n+1)^2}$	$\dfrac{a^2 n^2}{8b(n+1)^2}$
Worst case	Min R_n	Min L_n	Min M_n
	$-\dfrac{a^2(2n-1)}{2b(n+1)^2}$	$\dfrac{a^2(5-2n)}{2b(n+1)^2}$	$\dfrac{a^2(n^2-6n+5)}{8b(n+1)^2}$

there is some uncertainty about the welfare effects. For example, when antitrust replaces monopoly and n-firm equilibrium results, the possible changes in economic welfare form a bounded set on the interval (Min M_n, Max M_n). When M_n closely approximates Max M_n, welfare is always increased by the substitution. When M_n closely approximates Min M_n, the story is different. As Table 8.4 shows, in the worst case, Min M_n takes a positive sign when $n \geqq 6$ and a negative sign when $n \leqq 4$.

Some uncertainty about welfare effects there may be. Nevertheless, we know the limit values of M_n. Therefore, we can estimate the probability that, when antitrust replaces monopoly and an n-firm equilibrium results, an increase in economic welfare also results.

Let k designate the number of possible welfare outcomes when antitrust replaces monopoly. Let us assume that the probability that any single outcome will occur is $1/k$; that is, we assume a uniform distribution of M_n over the interval (Min M_n, Max M_n). There is no economic reason not to assume this distribution. Anyway, as we shall presently see, our results would be affected very little by the choice of a different probability distribution.

We know that Max $M_n > 0$ for every n. So long as Min $M_n \geqq 0$, there is no problem. Here $(Pr\ M_n \geqq 0) = 1$. When Min $M_n \leqq 0$, we have, with uniform distribution:

$$\Pr(M_n \geqq 0) = \text{Max } M_n / (\text{Max } M_n - \text{Min } M_n)$$

When the terms in the right-hand side are replaced by values from table 8.2, equation 8.2 reduces to

$$\Pr(M_n \geq 0) = n^2/(6n - 5)$$

An analogous series of operation yields, for almost all values of n,

$$\Pr(L_n \geq 0) = 1/2(n - 2)$$

And, of course,

$$\Pr(R_n > 0) = 0$$

The probability that the substitution of antitrust for something else will increase economic welfare (or at least not lower it) is given for various values of n in table 8.5.[23]

The meaning of table 8.5 is unmistakable: price theory can be more easily employed to discredit antitrust than to justify it. Is this conclusion really so surprising? The superiority of regulation (with marginal cost pricing) to antitrust has long been known. And the superiority of laissez-faire (with limit pricing) to antitrust has been strongly suggested by developments in the literature on limit pricing over the last twenty years.

Perhaps the most surprising result of our analysis is the quite respectable

TABLE 8.5. Probability That Antitrust Equals or Betters Various Alternatives

Number of Firms with Antitrust	Regulation (mc pricing)	Laissez-Faire (limit pricing)[a]	Monopoly
2	0.0	0.571	0.571
3	0.0	0.692	0.692
4	0.0	0.250	0.842
5	0.0	0.167	1.0
6	0.0	0.125	1.0
7	0.0	0.100	1.0
8	0.0	0.083	1.0
9	0.0	0.071	1.0
10	0.0	0.063	1.0
11	0.0	0.056	1.0
12	0.0	0.050	1.0

[a]For $n = 2$ and $n = 3$ limit price is monopoly price.

[23]Note that in table 8.5, when $n = 2$ and $n = 3$, the substitution of antitrust for monopoly has the same likelihood of increasing welfare as the substitution of antitrust for laissez-faire. This is because, for $n = 2$, $a/2 < 2a/(n + 1)$ and, for $n = 3$, $a/2 = 2a/(n + 1)$. That is, when $n = 2$ and $n = 3$, monopoly price is limit price since it is low enough to discourage entry.

showing of the monopoly alternative when antitrust can create only two or three viable firms. Thus

$$\Pr(M_n \geq 0) = 0.571 \text{ when } n = 2 \text{ and}$$
$$\Pr(M_n \geq 0) = 0.692 \text{ when } n = 3.$$

And these probabilities were computed on the assumption that the administrative cost of substituting antitrust for monopoly is null!

Table 8.5 confirms that regulation is always superior to antitrust.[24] The probability that the substitution of antitrust for laissez-faire will increase economic welfare is less than 0.3 for $n \geq 4$. As noted above, the probability that the substitution of antitrust for monopoly will increase economic welfare is 0.571 when $n = 2$ and 0.692 when $n = 3$. We do not get $\Pr(M_n \geq 0) = 1$ until $n \geq 5$.

Note that, in table 8.5, the probability that antitrust is "better" than monopoly increases as n increases over the interval $2 \leq n \leq 5$; whereas the probability that antitrust is better than laissez-faire decreases as n increases provided that $n \geq 4$. The reason for this discrepancy is that the difference between monopoly price and n-firm equilibrium price under antitrust becomes greater as n increases; whereas the difference between n-firm equilibrium price and limit price becomes smaller as n increases. (See figures 8.2 and 8.3.) As n goes from 2 to 3, this difference increases under limit pricing. This is because, as noted in footnote 23, for $n = 2$ and $n = 3$, monopoly price is also limit price.

Antitrust the Worst Choice?

FOR SOME years, this writer has argued that the absence of antitrust would produce not "monopoly" but limit pricing carried out by a multiplant firm or cartel. Multiplant firms and cartels that pool profits and assign output quotas are means by which production can be organized efficiently.[25] And if the efficient multiplant firm or cartel has no protection

---

[24]In the construction of table 8.5, the R_n's consistent with n-firm equilibrium have been treated as an open set on the interval (Min R_n, Max R_n). Thus, Min R_n—the value of R_n in best case antitrust—is not included in the set. Antitrust creates as much economic welfare as ideal regulation only at this best case limit.

[25]It is a simple, though not a popular, exercise in price theory to show that when an industry cannot support the number of firms needed for perfect competition, it will never be organized with maximum efficiency in the absence of a multiplant firm or cartel. For a necessary condition of maximum efficiency is that unit cost be minimized in all production units. When competition is less than perfect, this condition is achieved only with some form of command guidance. On cartel theory generally, see Donald Dewey, *The Theory of Imperfect Competition:*

against entry of new firms, its managers will presumably maximize profit by pricing to discourage entry. While this would seem to be "obviously" true, the idea of a limit price, though hardly new, must still fight for a place in price theory.[26] Economists now know, of course, that, in the absence of a legal barrier to entry, a high concentration ratio is unlikely to be associated with any close approximation to monopoly price. But, as yet, we find it difficult to discard the notion that we did so much to popularize: that a concentration ratio is a valid index of "monopoly power."[27] The courts, having no clear lead from price theory, have even fallen into the vulgar error of treating pricing to discourage entry as a monopolistic practice.

Without much trouble, we could show that for any economic model that posits free entry of firms, the equilibrium concentration ratio is a function of the legal system and optimum firm size in relation to magnitude of demand. Likewise, without much trouble, we could show that the profit rates and concentration ratios are simultaneously determined and that one in no sense "causes" the other. (As noted in footnote 22, when competition is less than perfect, free entry does not necessarily produce an equilibrium with zero profit; here, free entry merely imposes an upper bound on the set of profit rates that is consistent with equilibrium.) In short, a high concentration ratio is not, in any meaningful sense, a "barrier to entry." It is merely evidence that, given the constraints of law, technology, and demand, the industry cannot support more firms.

The policy implications of table 8.5 are quite startling. Antitrust comes at a cost, because it tends to create excess capacity. This it does by discouraging the price wars and mergers that would otherwise reduce the number of firms. This tendency to excess capacity is not inherent in any of the alternatives to antitrust. In fact, to the extent that the imperfect regulation and laissez-faire of the real world succeed in keeping down ex-

---

A Radical Reconstruction (1969), pp. 41–59; Don Patinkin, "Multi-plant Firms, Cartels, and Imperfect Competition," 61 *Q.J. Econ* 173 (1947); William Fellner, *Competition Among the Few*, (1949), pp. 200–210.

The most famous of American cartel cases, *Addyston Pipe & Steel Company et al. v. United States*, 175 U.S. 211 (1899) laid the basis for the per se rule against price fixing and has been almost universally praised over the years. Even by Robert Bork and Richard Posner! However, a recent reconsideration of the case strongly suggests that the cartel of castiron pipe producers condemned in this case served to increase economic welfare. George Bittlingmayer, "Price-Fixing and the Addyston Pipe Case," 5 *Research in Law and Economics* 57 (1982).

[26]Perfectly lucid descriptions of limit pricing appear as early as John B. Clark, *Essentials of Economic Theory*, (1907), pp. 380–81; and Alfred Marshall, *Industry and Trade* (1920), p. 397.

[27]No originality can be claimed for the complaint. For an earlier and more detailed version, see Harold Demsetz, "Economics as a Guide to Antitrust Regulation," 19 *J. Law Econ.* 371 (1976).

cess capacity, they may be preferable to antitrust, even though they lead to prices that have drifted upward toward the monopoly level.

It is generally assumed that real world regulation in particular is very far from ideal. Certainly this writer so believes. Unfortunately, the method usually chosen to carry out "deregulation"—relaxing entry controls while restricting mergers and discouraging cartels—is thoroughly suspect on welfare grounds. It is the perfect formula for creating excess capacity. Deregulation of air transportation has undoubtedly resulted in lower fares. Basic price theory leads us to believe that another result has been too many small planes flying too often.

A Pitfall Noted

THE ANALYSIS of this paper underscores another old truth often forgotten: the welfare consequences of substituting antitrust for monopoly and laissez-faire cannot be seen by looking only at what happens to prices, output, and profit rates. As tables 8.1 and 8.2 make clear, replacement of either system by antitrust always leads to lower prices and lower monopoly rent. Indeed, in our model, resort to antitrust completely eliminates monopoly rent no matter what happens to economic welfare. Clearly, consumer welfare, narrowly defined, is not the same thing as economic welfare.[28]

A Reassurance?

OUR CONCLUSIONS about the welfare effects of substituting antitrust for something else have been based upon the assumption that, for an n-firm equilibrium, these effects are uniformly distributed between a lower bound and an upper bound. These bounds (Min M_n, Max M_n etc.) are the important constraints. Little would change if a different probability dis-

---

[28]Robert Bork is a leading proponent of the view that the goal of antitrust ought to be consumer welfare, narrowly defined. He holds that an antitrust rule is acceptable only if price theory supports the presumption that it will increase output with an increase in output being, by definition, an increase in consumer welfare. *The Antitrust Paradox: A Policy at War with Itself* (1978), pp. 81–82.

Under our "ideal" antitrust, only output-increasing rules would be in force; thus it would always increase consumer welfare though, as we have found, by creating excess capacity it might at the same time, reduce economic welfare. Bork's output test is, I believe, perfectly defensible as a judicial rule of thumb since, for the present, it is too much to expect that courts should be concerned with such a rarified thing as the economist's distinction between economic welfare and consumer welfare. A judicial focus on a simple output test would at least discourage such welfare-reducing monstrosities as *Utah Pie Co. v. Continental Baking Co.*, 386 U.S. 685 (1967).

tribution were used. Whatever the distribution, ideal regulation is always better than antitrust (except at the limit of best case antitrust, where it is equally good). The probability that antitrust is better than laissez-faire is almost always less than 0.3; and provided that $n > 5$, antitrust is always better than monopoly. Suppose that a different probability distribution were assumed. The only result would be marginally to strengthen (or weaken) the case for replacing laissez-faire or monopoly with antitrust.

Economic Welfare and "Squandered Monopoly"

LEST WE appear to do less than justice to the case for antitrust, one further calculation should be made. In recent years, Gordon Tullock, Richard Posner, and others have suggested that the welfare loss of monopoly can be much greater than the dead-weight loss of any consumer surplus destroyed.[29] They point out that if a monopoly rent is to be had, rational people will invest resources to create, appropriate, and protect it; and that, at the limit, monopoly can induce a waste of resources equal to the monopoly rent gained.

In a world of regulated industries with entry controls, regulators seldom revoke franchises already issued and rather routinely renew franchises at expiration. Therefore, it seems likely that the magnitude of this induced waste is much exaggerated by popularizers of the idea. For example, the value of resources devoted by owners of television stations to cosseting their licenses (legal fees, public service broadcasts, etc.) is surely far less than the monopoly rents created for them by government policy. Still, to the extent that monopoly induces a waste of resources, the case for antitrust over monopoly is strengthened. Indeed, it can be shown that at the limit, when all monopoly rent has been frittered away in resource waste, the substitution of antitrust will *always* increase economic welfare.

Let S_n designate the welfare gain to be gotten by shifting to antitrust from squandered monopoly and Min S_n the minimum values that S_n can take. We show that antitrust is always better than squandered monopoly by proving the $\Pr(S_n > 0) \equiv 1$. To this end, we need only demonstrate that Min $S_n > 0$ for every n.

By definition Min S_n is the sum of Min M_n and the monopolist's economic rent, i.e., his total revenue minus his total cost. Using the information on worst case antitrust provided by tables 8.1 and 8.4 we have:

---

[29]See, for example, Gordon Tullock, "The Welfare Cost of Tariffs, Monopolies, and Theft," *Western Econ. J.* 224 (1964); or Richard A. Posner, "The Social Cost of Monopoly and Regulation," 83 *J. Pol. Econ.* 83 (1975).

$$\text{Min } S_n = \frac{a^2(n^2 - 6n + 5)}{8b(n + 1)^2} + \frac{a^2}{4b} - \frac{a^2}{b(n + 1)^2} \qquad (8.5)$$

or

$$\text{Min } S_n = \frac{a^2(3n^2 + 2n - 1)}{8b(n + 1)^2} \qquad (8.5a)$$

Thus, Min $S_n > 0$ for all values of n and economic welfare will always be increased by the substitution of antitrust for squandered monopoly.

Other Costs Noted

SO FAR, in assessing the welfare impacts of antitrust and its alternatives, we have ignored the costs of implementing them. When these costs are put into the picture, price theorists must either step aside in favor of econometricians or speak in generalities. Speaking in generalities, it seems safe to assume that the cost of implementing antitrust must be greater than the comparable cost of laissez-faire. To go no further, the number of American lawyers who are presently making a living out of antitrust almost certainly exceed by fivefold the combined total of practicing barristers and solicitors in Great Britain.

It is not so obvious how the cost of implementing antitrust compares with the cost of implementing monopoly or regulation aimed at marginal cost (or even average cost) pricing. Most economists, or at any rate most American economists, probably feel that the antitrust cost is lower. But we do not really know.

Antitrust and the Demand Function

SO FAR, our analysis has assumed that the industry's demand curve is linear. We chose to accept this restriction because a linear demand function greatly simplifies the algebra and because there was no obvious reason for not making use of this advantage. But let us be clear that the conclusion that "antitrust comes at a cost" does not depend upon anything so trivial as the exact slope of a demand curve. Our analysis could be conducted with any differentiable demand function that yields a total revenue maximum for some positive rate of output. Introducing nonlinear demand functions would deprive our analysis of much of its precision (and simplicity) without telling us anything new or interesting about the welfare tradeoffs of antitrust and its alternatives.

For the record, we can easily show that the more convex the demand curve, the greater the welfare gain to be had (or the smaller the welfare loss to be suffered) by substituting antitrust for monopoly or laissez-faire. Likewise, the more concave the demand curve, the smaller the welfare gain to be had (or the greater the welfare loss to be suffered) from such substitutions.[30] There would seem to be no point in pursuing the implications of curvature in greater detail. It is doubtful that even the most fervent trustbuster would try to strengthen the case for antitrust by arguing that real world demand curves are highly convex. Certainly there is no extant body of empirical or theoretical work that would support such a view.

Final Thoughts

HOW SERIOUSLY should the above results be taken? The answer depends, of course, upon the role assigned to price theory and conventional welfare criteria in antitrust policy. If one believes that these are the only acceptable instruments for distinguishing good from bad in antitrust, the results would seem to be quite disturbing. Price theory and conventional welfare criteria can provide libertarians of the Von Mises school and market socialists of the Oskar Lange school with a great deal of intellectual ammunition and spiritual comfort. They can provide little of either to friends of antitrust.

If one does not require the case for antitrust to be grounded only in price theory and welfare economics, our results can be viewed as interesting but without decisive significance for policy. As wise elders have often cautioned, economic progress is a much more important desideratum

---

[30]Let S denote any set of continuous demand functions $\Phi(x)$ such that, for values of p^* and x^* $(p^* > 0, x^* > 0)$ [i] $\Phi(x^*) = 0$ [ii] $\Phi(0) = p^*$ and [iii] on the interval $(0,x^*)$ the sign of $\Phi''(x)$ does not change. Let marginal revenue be given by:

$$m = d[x\Phi(x)]/dx.$$

Let the concavity of $\Phi(x)$ be given by $e = \int_0^{x*} \Phi(x) - 1/2\, p^*x^*$. Let $p_i = \Phi_i(x)\epsilon S$ and $p_j = \Phi_j(x)\epsilon S$.

Then for every $x\,(0 < x < x^*)$, if $e_i > e_j$, we have [i] $\Phi_i(x) > \Phi_j(x)$ and [ii] $m_i > m_j$.

A monopolist is presumed to equate marginal cost and marginal revenue. Therefore, for any given cost function, the more concave the industry demand curve, i.e., the greater the value of e, the greater will be equilibrium output under monopoly; and the smaller will be the welfare gain (or the greater will be the welfare loss) obtainable by substituting antitrust for monopoly.

An analogous line of argument can be used to show that the more concave the demand curve, the smaller will be the welfare gain to be had (or the greater the welfare loss to be suffered) by substituting antitrust for laissez-faire.

than efficient resource allocation.[31] Certainly, it is a logical possibility that antitrust may create market structures that, at the same time, reduce economic welfare and raise the rate of economic progress. As yet, we have neither theoretical nor empirical work that allows us to estimate the likelihood that antitrust will have this result.[32] The most we can say is that no good evidence has been produced to show that antitrust reduces the rate of economic progress.

Still, suppose that one day the economic effects of antitrust will be revealed as totally perverse, i.e., that it will be found to reduce both economic welfare and the rate of economic progress. All of the so-called noneconomic arguments for the policy will remain. (Small business builds character, economic decentralization improves political democracy, etc.) It is, after all, a professional conceit to believe that the main object of antitrust is (or should be) an increase in that rarefied thing that economist have defined as economic welfare.

If the goals of antitrust are to be inferred from what judges and legislators do (forget what they say), it is clear that its paramount goal, from 1890 onward, has been the preservation and promotion of decentralized decision-making, subject to two main constraints. Economic efficiency must not be jeopardized in any gross and obvious way, eg., by using divestiture to create firms with poor chances of survival. Established stockholder and employee interests must not be too rudely disturbed. For better or worse, great corporate size scares a great many people in this country.[33] "Monopoly power" divorced from great corporate size scares hardly anybody and, indeed, mostly goes unnoticed. In this country, the suspicion of centralized decision-making extends far beyond the large corporation—to

[31]Notably, John M. Clark, *Competition as a Dynamic Process* (1961), and Joseph Schumpeter, *Capitalism, Socialism, and Democracy*, 3d ed. (1950).

[32]For an appraisal of the work on what we know (and suspect) about the tie between technological progress and market structure, see Morton I. Kamien and Nancy L. Schwartz, *Market Structure and Innovation* (1982).

[33]Admittedly, the recent break-up of the Bell System may inflict injuries on workers and investors that contradict the above generalizations. I think it fair to say that, if this result comes to pass, it can be attributed more to management's miscalculation about its ability to compete in unregulated markets (and, hence, its willingness to accept the actual consent decree) than to the court's determination to destroy the monopoly rents of workers and stockholders. (In defense of the managers' decision to settle, lawyers will hasten to point out that they had to weigh the value of a consent decree that expressly provided some protection against private treble damage suits against the probability of an unfavorable ruling that would have given third parties a prima facie case against the Bell System. *United States v. Western Electric Co., Inc., and American Telephone and Telegraph Co.,* 1982–2 Trade Cases 72,555 at 72,558). My own expectation is that if workers and stockholders ultimately suffer severe losses as a result of the Bell System dissolution, the country will not see a comparable adventure in trust-busting for many years.

government, political parties, churches, universities, labor unions, and the money and credit system. Why this is so is, of course, a subject much too vast for this paper.

These concluding thoughts are not meant to depreciate the value of price theory in analyzing antitrust issues. It provides the most powerful set of tools that we have for identifying and estimating tangible costs and benefits. So long as we are thinking straight, our willingness to sacrifice economic welfare to achieve other goals is necessarily affected by such calculations.

Will it greatly matter in Congress and the courts if economists conclude that the price theory of the textbooks provides virtually no support for antitrust? At first glance, an affirmative answer would seem to be out of the question. No political leader with any hope of office or influence dares to speak against antitrust. Few American economists and even fewer American lawyers ever bother to consider what the American economy would be like without it; and the policy now has the respectability conferred by age and the support of an organized constituency in the large and prosperous Antitrust Bar. For the record, antitrust was born in the populist turbulence of the last century and gained its great 1911 victories without the benefit of price theory or price theorists.[34]

Still, as the recent movement toward deregulation in transportation and communications should remind us, ideas can matter in the long run. The movement is directly traceable to the discrediting of the Brandeis-Sharfman case for public utility regulation that began at the University of Chicago in the 1930s. The support belatedly given to antitrust by economists after 1900 did have one obvious and possibly important result: it conferred intellectual respectability. If this respectability is taken away, the ultimate consequence cannot be predicted. Presumably, the disenchantment of economists with antitrust will have some effect; even the most pessimistic of us cannot believe that his work counts for nothing in the forum. The only reasonable prophecy is that our loss of faith in antitrust will cause the alternatives—and not only those considered in this paper—to be more closely examined. That could be a most interesting development.

---

[34] *Standard Oil Co. of New Jersey v. United States,* 221 U.S. 1 (1911); *United States v. American Tobacco Co.* et al., 221, U.S. 106 (1911).

Index